ISBN 978-1-333-63694-4
PIBN 10529376

1 MONTH OF
FREE
READING

at

www.ForgottenBooks.com

By purchasing this book you are eligible for one month membership to ForgottenBooks.com, giving you unlimited access to our entire collection of over 700,000 titles via our web site and mobile apps.

To claim your free month visit:
www.forgottenbooks.com/free529376

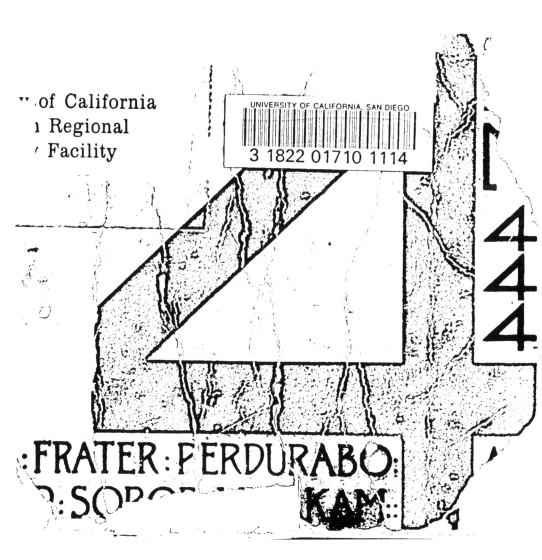

: FRATER : FERDURABO :

: SO   KAM :

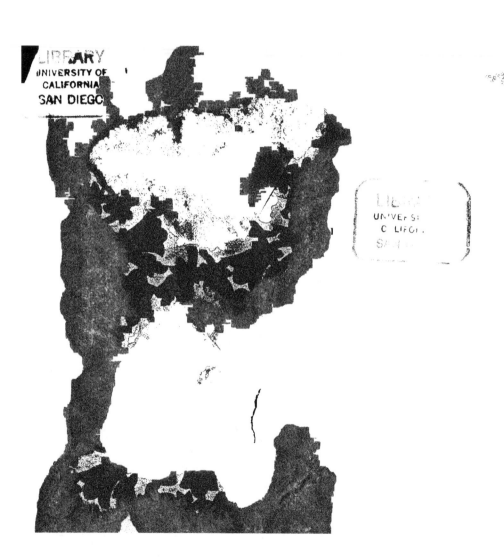

PRICE
FOUR TANNERS
OR
TWO SHILLINGS
NET
LONDON : WIELAND
33 AVENUE STUDIOS
(76 FULHAM ROAD)
Tel: 2632 Ken.

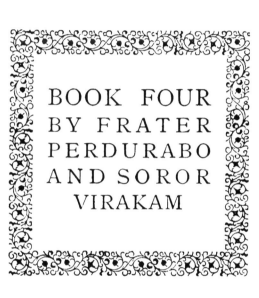

BOOK FOUR
BY FRATER
PERDURABO
AND SOROR
VIRAKAM

Issued by order of
the GREAT WHITE
BROTHERHOOD
known as the A∴ A ·

Witness our Seal,

N ∴

Praemonstrator-General.

A NOTE

THIS book is intentionally *not* the work of Frater Perdurabo. Experience shows that his writing is too concentrated, too abstruse, too occult, for ordinary minds to apprehend. It is thought that this record of disjointed fragments of his casual conversation may prove alike more intelligible and more convincing, and at least provide a preliminary study which will enable the student to attack his real work from a standpoint of some little general knowledge and understanding of his ideas, and of the form in which he figures them.

Part II, "Magick," is more advanced in style than Part I; the student is expected to know a little of the literature of the subject, and to be able to take an intelligent view of it. This part is, however, really explanatory of Part I, which is a crude outline sketch only.

If both parts are thoroughly studied and understood, the pupil will have obtained a real grasp of all the fundamentals and essentials of both Magick and Mysticism.

I wrote this book down from Frater Perdurabo's dictation at the Villa Caldarazzo, Posilippo, Naples, where I was studying under him, a villa actually prophesied to us long before we reached Naples by that Brother of the A∴ A∴ who appeared to me in Zürich. Any point which was obscure to me was cleared up in some new discourse (the discourses have consequently been re-arranged). Before printing, the whole work was read by several persons of rather less that average intelligence, and any point not quite clear even to them has been elucidated.

May the whole Path now be plain to all!

Frater Perdurabo is the most honest of all the great religious teachers. Others have said: "Believe me!" He says: "*Don't* believe me!" He does not ask for followers; would despise and refuse them. He wants an independent and self-reliant body of students to follow out their own methods of research. If he can save them time and trouble by giving a few useful "tips," his work will have been done to his own satisfaction.

Those who have wished men to believe in them were absurd. A persuasive tongue or pen, or an efficient sword, with rack and stake, produced this "belief," which is contrary to, and destructive of, all real religious experience.

The whole life of Frater Perdurabo is now devoted to seeing that you obtain this living experience of Truth for, by, and in yourselves!

SOROR VIRAKAM (Mary d'Este Sturges).

Frater Perdurabo is always ready to give personal instruction, free of all charge, to any person who may apply to him. Letters should be *registered*, and addressed to him, care of the publishers,

WIELAND AND CO.,
33, AVENUE STUDIOS
(76, FULHAM ROAD),
SOUTH KENSINGTON,
LONDON, S.W.

ERRATA

Half-title, *after* " MAGICK " *insert* " (THEORY)."

Page 15, line 11, *for* " a moral lesson " *read* " several moral lessons."

Page 42, note, line 2, *omit* " leading."

Page 96, line 15, *for* " Death " *read* " Daäth."

Page 127, line 13, *for* " us " *read* " a man."

Page 166, line 12, *after* " and " *insert* " whose third ingredient is."

Order Form, *for* " [" RITUAL "] " *read* " MAGICK (PRACTICE)."

PART II—MAGICK

PRELIMINARY REMARKS

THE MAGICIAN

IN HIS ROBE AND CROWN, ARMED WITH WAND, CUP, SWORD,
PANTACLE, BELL, BOOK, AND HOLY OIL.

CEREMONIAL MAGICK,[1]

THE TRAINING FOR MEDITATION

PRELIMINARY REMARKS

HITHERTO we have spoken only of the mystic path; and we have kept particularly to the practical exoteric side of it. Such difficulties as we have mentioned have been purely natural obstacles. For example, the great question of the surrender of the self, which bulks so largely in most mystical treatises, has not been referred to at all. We have said only what a man must do; we have not considered at all what that doing may involve. The rebellion of the will against the terrible discipline of meditation has not been discussed; one may now devote a few words to it.

There is no limit to what theologians call "wickedness." Only by experience can the student discover the ingenuity of the mind in trying to escape from control. He is perfectly safe so long as he sticks to meditation, doing no more and no less than that

---

[1] The old spelling MAGICK has been adopted throughout in order to distinguish the Science of the Magi from all its counterfeits.

which we have prescribed; but the mind will probably not let him remain in that simplicity. This fact is the root of all the legends about the "Saint" being tempted by the "Devil." Consider the parable of Christ in the Wilderness, where he is tempted to use his magical power, to do anything but the thing that should be done. These attacks on the will are as bad as the thoughts which intrude upon Dharana. It would almost seem as if one could not successfully practice meditation until the will had become so strong that no force in the Universe could either bend or break it. **Before concentrating the lower principle, the mind, one must concentrate the higher principle, the Will.** Failure to understand this has destroyed the value of all attempts to teach "Yoga," "Menticulture," "New Thought," and the like.

There are methods of training the will, by which it is easy to check one's progress.

Every one knows the force of habit. Every one knows that if you keep on acting in a particular way, that action becomes easier, and at last absolutely natural.

All religions have devised practices for this purpose. If you keep on praying with your lips long enough, you will one day find yourself praying in your heart.

The whole question has been threshed out and organized

by wise men of old; they have made a Science of Life complete and perfect; and they have given to it the name of **MAGICK.** It is the chief secret of the Ancients, and if the keys have never been actually lost, they have certainly been little used.[1]

Again, the confusion of thought caused by the ignorance of the people who did not understand it has discredited the whole subject. It is now our task to re-establish this science in its perfection.

To do this we must criticize the Authorities; some of them have made it too complex, others have completely failed in such simple matters as coherence. Many of the writers are empirics, still more mere scribes, while by far the largest class of all is composed of stupid charlatans.

We shall consider a simple form of magick, harmonized from many systems old and new, describing the various weapons of the Magician and the furniture of his temple. We shall explain to what each really corresponds, and discuss the construction and the use of everything.

The Magician works in a *Temple*; the Universe, which is (be it remembered!) conterminous with himself.[2] In this temple a *Circle* is drawn upon the floor for the limitation of his working. This circle is

---

[1] The holders of those keys have always kept very quiet about it. This has been especially necessary in Europe, because of the dominance of persecuting churches.

[2] By "yourself" you mean the contents of your consciousness. All without does not exist for you.

protected by divine names, the influences on which he relies to keep out hostile thoughts. Within the circle stands an *Altar*, the solid basis on which he works, the foundation of all. Upon the Altar are his *Wand*, *Cup*, *Sword*, and *Pantacle*, to represent his Will, his Understanding, his Reason, and the lower parts of his being, respectively. On the Altar, too, is a phial of *Oil*, surrounded by a *Scourge*, a *Dagger*, and a *Chain*, while above the Altar hangs a *Lamp*. The Magician wears a *Crown*, a single *Robe*, and a *Lamen*, and he bears a *Book* of Conjurations and a *Bell*.

The oil consecrates everything that is touched with it; it is his aspiration; all acts performed in accordance with that are holy. The scourge tortures him; the dagger wounds him; the chain binds him. It is by virtue of these three that his aspiration remains pure, and is able to consecrate all other things. He wears a crown to affirm his lordship, his divinity; a robe to symbolize silence, and a lamen to declare his work. The book of spells or conjurations is his magical record, his Karma. In the East is the *Magick Fire*, in which all burns up at last.[1]

We will now consider each of these matters in detail.

---

[1] He needs nothing else but the apparatus here described for invocation, by which he calls down that which is above him and within him; but for evocations, by which he calls forth that which is below him and without him, he may place a triangle without the circle.

THE TEMPLE

CHAPTER I

THE TEMPLE

THE Temple represents the external Universe. The Magician must take it as he finds it, so that it is of no particular shape; yet we find written, Liber VII, vi, 2: "We made us a Temple of stones in the shape of the Universe, even as thou didst wear openly and I concealed." This shape is the Vesica Piscis; but it is only the greatest of the Magicians who can thus fashion the Temple. There may, however, be some choice of rooms; this refers to the power of the Magician to reincarnate in a suitable body.

THE CIRCLE

THE CIRCLE

CHAPTER II

THE Circle announces the Nature of the Great Work. Though the Magician has been limited in his choice of room, he is more or less able to choose what part of the room he will work in. He will consider convenience and possibility. His circle should not be too small and cramp his movements; it should not be so large that he has long distances to traverse. Once the circle is made and consecrated, the Magician must not leave it, or even lean outside, lest he be destroyed by the hostile forces that are without.

He chooses a circle rather than any other lineal figure for many reasons; *e.g.*,

1. He affirms thereby his identity with the infinite.

2. He affirms the equal balance of his working; since all points on the circumference are equidistant from the centre.

3. He affirms the limitation implied by his devotion to the Great Work. He no longer wanders about aimlessly in the world.

The centre of this circle is the centre of the Tau of ten squares which is in the midst, as shown in the illustration. The Tau and the circle together make one form of the Rosy Cross, the uniting of subject and object which is the Great Work, and which is symbolized sometimes as this cross and circle, sometimes as the Lingam-Yoni, sometimes as the Ankh or Crux Ansata, sometimes by the Spire and Nave of a church or temple, and sometimes as a marriage feast, mystic marriage, spiritual marriage, "chymical nuptials," and in a hundred other ways. Whatever the form chosen, it is the symbol of the Great Work.

This place of his working therefore declares the nature and object of the Work. Those persons who have supposed that the use of these symbols implied worship of the generative organs, merely attributed to the sages of every time and country minds of a calibre equal to their own.

The Tau is composed of ten squares for the ten Sephiroth.[1] About this Tau is escribed a triangle, which is inscribed in the great Circle; but of the triangle nothing is actually marked but the three corners, the areas defined by the cutting of the lines bounding this triangle. This triangle is only visible in the parts which are common to two of the

---

[1] The Ten Sephiroth are the Ten Units. In one system of classification (see " 777 ") these are so arranged, and various ideas are so attributed to them, that they have been made to mean anything. The more you know, the more these numbers mean to you.

sides; they have therefore the shape of the diamond, one form of the Yoni. The significance of this is too complex for our simple treatise; it may be studied in Crowley's " Berashith."

The size of the whole figure is determined by the size of one square of the Tau. And the size of this square is that of the base of the Altar, which is placed upon Malkuth. It will follow then that, in spite of the apparent freedom of the Magician to do anything he likes, he is really determined absolutely; for as the Altar must have a base proportionate to its height, and as that height must be convenient for the Magician, the size of the whole will depend upon his own stature. It is easy to draw a moral lesson from these considerations. We will merely indicate this one, that the scope of any man's work depends upon his own original genius. Even the size of the weapons must be determined by necessary proportion. The exceptions to this rule are the Lamp, which hangs from the roof, above the centre of the Circle, above the square of Tiphereth; and the Oil, whose phial is so small that it will suit any altar.

On the Circle are inscribed the Names of God; the Circle is of green, and the names are in flaming vermilion, of the same colour as the Tau. Without the Circle are nine pentagrams equidistant,[1] in the

[1] Some magicians prefer seven lamps, for the seven Spirits of God that are before the Throne. Each stands in a heptagram, and in each angle of the heptagram is a

centre of each of which burns a small Lamp; these are the "Fortresses upon the Frontiers of the Abyss." See the eleventh Aethyr, Liber 418 ("Equinox V"). **They keep off those forces of darkness which might otherwise break in.**

The names of God form a further protection. The Magician may consider what names he will use; but each name should in some way symbolise this Work in its method and accomplishment. It is impossible here to enter into this subject fully; the discovery or construction of suitable names might occupy the most learned Qabalist for many years.

These nine lamps were originally candles made of human fat, the fat of enemies[1] slain by the Magician; they thus served as warnings to any hostile force of what might be expected if it caused trouble. To-day such candles are difficult to procure; and it is perhaps simpler to use beeswax. The honey has been taken by the Magician; nothing is left of the toil of all those hosts of bees but the mere shell, the fuel of light. This beeswax is also used in the construction of the Pantacle, and this

letter, so that the seven names (see "Equinox VII") are spelt out. But this is a rather different symbolism. Of course in ordinary specialised working the number of lamps depends on the nature of the work, *e.g.*, three for works of Saturn, eight for works Mercurial, and so on.

[1] Or sometimes of "birth-strangled babes," *i.e.*, of thoughts slain ere they could arise into consciousness.

forms a link between the two symbols. The Pantacle is the food of the Magus; and some of it he gives up in order to give light to that which is without. For these lights are only apparently hostile to intrusion; they serve to illuminate the Circle and the Names of God, and so to bring the first and outmost symbols of initiation within the view of the profane.

These candles stand upon pentagrams, which symbolize Geburah, severity, and give protection; but also represent the microcosm, the four elements crowned by Spirit, the Will of man perfected in its aspiration to the Higher. They are placed outside the Circle to attract the hostile forces, to give them the first inkling of the Great Work, which they too must some day perform.

THE ALTAR

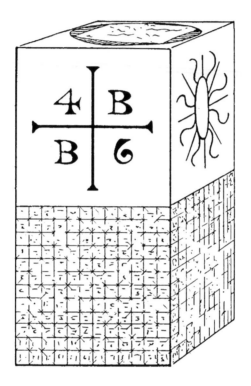

THE ALTAR. SIDE DESIGNS FROM DR. DEE, AS IN EQUINOX VII.

CHAPTER III

THE Altar represents the solid basis of the work, the fixed Will[1] of the Magician; and the law under which he works. Within this altar everything is kept, since everything is subject to law. Except the Lamp.

According to some authorities the Altar should be made of oak to represent the stubbornness and rigidity of law; others would make it of Acacia, for Acacia is the symbol of resurrection.

The Altar is a double cube, which is a rough way of symbolizing the Great Work; for the doubling of the cube, like the squaring of the circle, was one of the great problems of antiquity. The surface of this Altar is composed of ten squares. The top is Kether, and the

---

[1] It represents the extension of Will. Will is the Dyad (see section on the Wand); $2 \times 2 = 4$. So the altar is foursquare, and also its ten squares show 4. $10 = 1 + 2 + 3 + 4$.

bottom Malkuth. The height of the Altar is equal to the height above the ground of the navel of the Magician. The Altar is connected with the Ark of the Covenant, Noah's Ark, the nave (*navis*, a ship) of the Church, and many other symbols of antiquity, whose symbolism has been well worked out in an anonymous book called "The Canon," (Elkin Mathews), which should be studied carefully before constructing the Altar.

For this Altar must embody the Magician's knowledge of the laws of Nature, which are the laws through which he works.

He should endeavour to make geometrical constructions to symbolize cosmic measurements. For example, he may take the two diagonals as (say) the diameter of the sun. Then the side of the altar will be found to have a length equal to some other cosmic measure, a vesica drawn on the side some other, a "rood cross" within the vesica yet another. Each Magician should work out his own system of symbolism—and he need not confine himself to cosmic measurements. He might, for example, find some relation to express the law of inverse squares.

The top of the Altar shall be covered with gold, and on this gold should be engraved some such figure as the Holy Oblation, or the New Jerusalem, or, if he have the skill, the Microcosm of Vitruvius, of which we give illustrations.

On the sides of the Altar are also sometimes drawn the great tablets

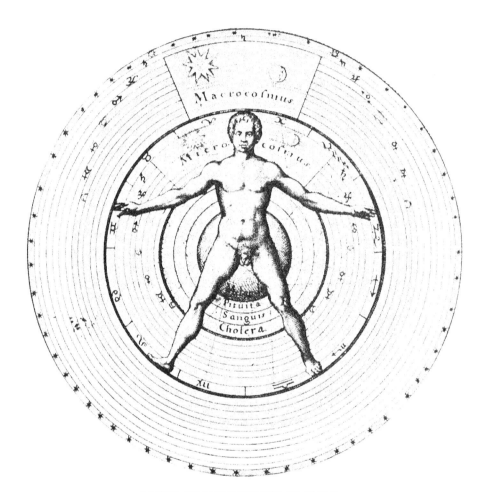

DESIGN SUITABLE FOR TOP OF ALTAR

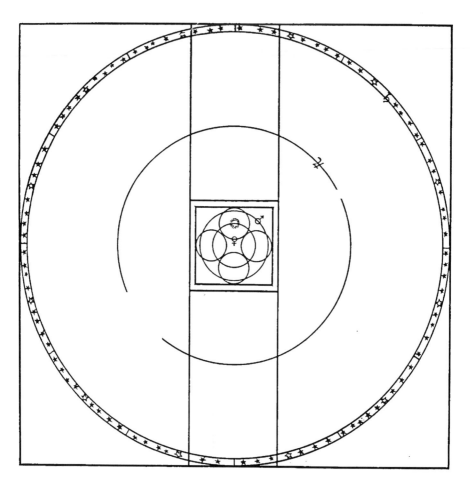

THE HOLY OBLATION

of the elements, and the sigils of the holy elemental kings, as shown in The Equinox, No. VII; for these are syntheses of the forces of Nature. Yet these are rather special than general symbols, and this book purports to treat only of the grand principles of working.

THE SCOURGE, THE DAGGER, AND THE CHAIN

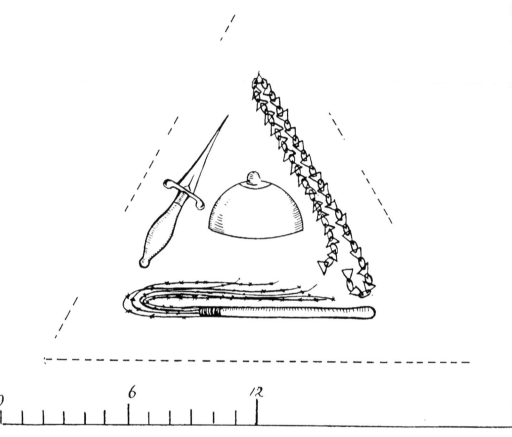

THE SCOURGE, THE DAGGER, AND THE CHAIN; ENCLOSING THE PHIAL FOR THE HOLY OIL.

CHAPTER IV

THE SCOURGE, THE DAGGER, AND THE CHAIN

THE Scourge, the Dagger, and the Chain, represent the three alchemical principles of Sulphur, Mercury, and Salt. These are not the substances which we now call by these names; they represent "principles," whose operations chemists have found it more convenient to explain in other ways. But Sulphur represents the energy of things, Mercury their fluidity, Salt their fixity. They are analogous to Fire, Air and Water; but they mean rather more, for they represent something deeper and subtler, and yet more truly active. An almost exact analogy is given by the three Gunas of the Hindus · Sattvas, Rajas, and Tamas. Sattvas is Mercury, equable, calm, clear; Rajas is Sulphur, active, excitable, even fierce; Tamas is Salt, thick sluggish, heavy, dark.[1]

But Hindu philosophy is so occupied with the main idea that only the Absolute is worth anything, that it tends to consider these Gunas

[1] There is a long description of these three Gunas in the Bhagavadgita.

(even Sattvas) as evil. This is a correct view, but only from above; and we prefer, if we are truly wise, to avoid this everlasting wail which characterizes the thought of the Indian peninsula: "Everything is sorrow," etc. Accepting their doctrine of the two phases of the Absolute, we must, if we are to be consistent, class the two phases together, either as good or as bad; if one is good and the other bad we are back again in that duality, to avoid which we invented the Absolute.

The Christian idea that sin was worth while because salvation was so much more worth while, that redemption is so splendid that innocence was well lost, is more satisfactory. St. Paul says: "Where sin abounded, there did grace much more abound. Then shall we do evil that good may come? God forbid." But (clearly!) it is exactly what God Himself did, or why did He create Satan with the germ of his "fall" in him?

Instead of condemning the three qualities outright, we should consider them as parts of a sacrament. This particular aspect of the Scourge, the Dagger, and the Chain, suggests the sacrament of penance.

The Scourge is Sulphur: its application excites our sluggish natures; and it may further be used as an instrument of correction, to castigate rebellious volitions. It is applied to the Nephesh the Animal Soul, the natural desires.

The **Dagger** is Mercury: it is used to calm too great heat, by the letting of blood; and it is this weapon which is plunged into the side or heart of the Magician to fill the Holy Cup. Those faculties which come between the appetites and the reason are thus dealt with.

The **Chain is Salt**: it serves to bind the wandering thoughts; and for this reason is placed about the neck of the Magician, where Daäth is situated.

These instruments also remind us of pain, death, and bondage. Students of the gospel will recollect that in the martyrdom of Christ these three were used, the dagger being replaced by the nails.[1]

The Scourge should be made with a handle of iron; the lash is composed of nine strands of fine copper wire, in each of which are twisted small pieces of lead. Iron represents severity, copper love, and lead austerity.

The Dagger is made of steel inlaid with gold; and the hilt is also golden.

The chain is made of soft iron. It has 333 links.[2]

---

[1] This is true of all magical instruments. The Hill of Golgotha is the circle, and the Cross the Tau. Christ had robe, crown, sceptre, etc.; this thesis should one day be fully worked out.

[2] See The Equinox, No. V, " The Vision and the Voice ": Xth Aethyr.

It is now evident why these weapons are grouped around the phial of clear crystal in which is kept the Holy Oil.

The Scourge keeps the aspiration keen: the Dagger expresses the determination to sacrifice all; and the Chain restricts any wandering.

We may now consider the Holy Oil itself.

THE HOLY OIL

CHAPTER V

THE Holy Oil is the Aspiration of the Magician; it is that which consecrates him to the performance of the Great Work; and such is its efficacy that it also consecrates all the furniture of the Temple and the instruments thereof. It is also the grace or chrism; for this aspiration is not ambition; it is a quality bestowed from above. For this reason the Magician will anoint first the top of his head before proceeding to consecrate the lower centres in their turn.

This oil is of a pure golden colour; and when placed upon the skin it should burn and thrill through the body with an intensity as of fire. It is the pure light translated into terms of desire. It is not the Will of the Magician, the desire of the lower to reach the higher; but it is that spark of the higher in the Magician which wishes to unite the lower with itself.

Unless therefore the Magician be first anointed with this oil, all his work will be wasted and evil.

D

This oil is compounded of four substances. The basis of all is the oil of the olive. The olive is, traditionally, the gift of Minerva, the Wisdom of God, the Logos. In this are dissolved three other oils; oil of myrrh, oil of cinnamon, oil of galangal. The Myrrh is attributed to Binah, the Great Mother, who is both the understanding of the Magician and that sorrow and compassion which results from the contemplation of the Universe. The Cinnamon represents Tiphereth, the Sun—the Son, in whom Glory and Suffering are identical. The Galangal represents both Kether and Malkuth, the First and the Last, the One and the Many, since in this Oil they are One.

These oils taken together represent therefore the whole Tree of Life. The ten Sephiroth are blended into the perfect gold.

This Oil cannot be prepared from crude myrrh, cinnamon, and galangal. The attempt to do so only gives a brown mud with which the oil will not mix. These substances must be themselves refined into pure oils before the final combination.

This perfect Oil is most penetrating and subtle. Gradually it will spread itself, a glistening film, over every object in the Temple. Each of these objects will then flame in the light of the Lamp. This Oil is like that which was in the widow's cruse: it renews and multiplies itself miraculously; its perfume fills the whole Temple; it is the soul of which the grosser perfume is the body.

35

The phial which contains the Oil should be of clear rock crystal, and some magicians have fashioned it in the shape of the female breast, for that it is the true nourishment of all that lives. For this reason also it has been made of mother-of-pearl and stoppered with a ruby.

THE WAND

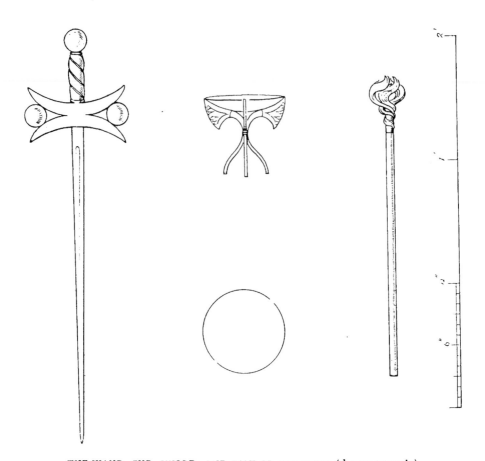

THE WAND, CUP, SWORD, AND DISK OR PANTACLE (drawn to scale).

CHAPTER VI

THE WAND

THE Magical Will is in its essence twofold, for it presupposes a beginning and an end; to will to be a thing is to admit that you are not that thing.

Hence to will anything but the supreme thing, is to wander still further from it—any will but that to give up the self to the Beloved is Black Magick—yet this surrender is so simple an act that to our complex minds it is the most difficult of all acts; and hence training is necessary. Further, the Self surrendered must not be less than the All-Self; one must not come before the altar of the Most High with an impure or an imperfect offering. As it is written in Liber LXV, "To await Thee is the end, not the beginning."

This training may lead through all sorts of complications, varying according to the nature of the student, and hence it may be necessary for him at any moment to will all sorts of things which to others might seem unconnected with the goal. Thus it is not *à priori* obvious why a billiard player should need a file.

Since, then, we may want *anything*, let us see to it that our will is strong enough to obtain anything we want without loss of time.

It is therefore necessary to develop the will to its high-est point, even though the last task but one is the total sur-render of this will. Partial surrender of an imperfect will is of no account in Magick.

The will being a lever, a fulcrum is necessary; this fulcrum is the main aspiration of the student to attain. All wills which are not de-pendent upon this principal will are so many leakages; they are like fat to the athlete.

The majority of the people in this world are ataxic; they cannot co-ördinate their mental muscles to make a purposed movement. They have no real will, only a set of wishes, many of which contradict others. The victim wobbles from one to the other (and it is no less wobbling because the movements may occasionally be very violent) and at the end of life the movements cancel each other out. Nothing has been achieved; except the one thing of which the victim is not conscious: the destruction of his own character, the confirming of indecision. Such an one is torn limb from limb by Choronzon.

How then is the will to be trained? All these wishes, whims, caprices, inclinations, tendencies, appetites, must be detected, examined, judged by the standard of whether they help or hinder the main purpose, and treated accordingly.

Vigilance and courage are obviously required. I was about to add self-denial, in deference to conventional speech; but how could I call that self-denial which is merely denial of those things which hamper the self? It is not suicide to kill the germs of malaria in one's blood.

Now there are very great difficulties to be overcome in the training of the mind. Perhaps the greatest is forgetfulness, which is probably the worst form of what the Buddhists call ignorance. Special practices for training the memory may be of some use as a preliminary for persons whose memory is naturally poor. In any case the Magical Record prescribed for Probationers by the A.·.A.·. is useful and necessary.

Above all the practices of Liber III must be done again and again, for these practices develop not only vigilance but those inhibiting centres in the brain which are, according to some psychologists, the mainspring of the mechanism by which civilized man has raised himself above the savage.

So far it has been spoken, as it were, in the negative. Aaron's rod has become a serpent, and swallowed the serpents of the other Magicians· it is now necessary to turn it once more into a rod.[1]

_____

[1] As everyone knows, the word used in Exodus for a Rod of Almond is מטה השקד,

This Magical Will is the wand in your hand by which the Great Work is accomplished, by which the Daughter is not merely set upon the throne of the Mother, but assumed into the Highest.[1]

The Magick Wand is thus the principal weapon of the Magus; and the *name* of that wand is the Magical Oath.

The will being twofold is in Chokmah, who is the Logos, the word; hence some have said that **the word is the will.** Thoth the Lord of Magic is also the Lord of Speech; Hermes the messenger bears the Caduceus.

Word should express will: hence **the Mystic Name of the Probationer is the expression of his highest Will.**

There are, of course, few Probationers who understand themselves sufficiently to be able to formulate this will to themselves, and therefore at the end of their probation they choose a new name.

---

adding to 463. Now 400 is Tau, the path leading from Malkuth to Yesod. Sixty is Samekh, the path leading leading from Yesod to Tiphereth; and 3 is Gimel, the path leading thence to Kether. The whole rod therefore gives the paths from the Kingdom to the Crown.

[1] In one, the best, system of Magick, the Absolute is called the Crown, God is called the Father, the Pure Soul is called the Mother, the Holy Guardian Angel is called the Son, and the Natural Soul is called the Daughter. The Son purifies the Daughter by wedding her; she thus becomes the Mother, the uniting of whom with the Father absorbs all into the Crown. See Liber CDXVIII.

It is convenient therefore for the student to express his will by taking Magical Oaths.

Since such an oath is irrevocable it should be well considered; and it is better not to take any oath permanently; because with increase of understanding may come a perception of the incompatibility of the lesser oath with the greater.

This is indeed almost certain to occur, and it must be remembered that as the whole essence of the will is its one-pointedness,[1] a dilemma of this sort is the worst in which the Magus can find himself.

Another great point in this consideration of Magick Vows is to keep them in their proper place. They must be taken for a clearly defined purpose, a clearly understood purpose, and they must never be allowed to go beyond it.

It is a virtue in a diabetic not to eat sugar, but only in reference to his own condition. It is not a virtue of universal import. Elijah said on one occasion: "I do well to be angry;" but such occasions are rare.

Moreover, one man's meat is another man's poison. An oath of poverty might be very useful for a man who was unable intelligently to use his wealth for the single end proposed; to another it would be

[1] The Top of the Wand is in Kether—which is one; and the Qliphoth of Kether are the Thaumiel, opposing heads that rend and devour each other.

simply stripping himself of energy, causing him to waste his time over trifles.

There is no power which cannot be pressed into the service of the Magical Will: it is only the temptation to value that power for itself which offends.

One does not say: "Cut it down; why cumbereth it the ground?" unless repeated prunings have convinced the gardener that the growth must always be a rank one.

"If thine hand offend thee, cut it off!" is the scream of a weakling. If one killed a dog the first time it misbehaved itself, not many would pass the stage of puppyhood.

The best vow, and that of most universal application, is the vow of Holy Obedience; for not only does it lead to perfect freedom, but is a training in that surrender which is the last task.

It has this great value, that it never gets rusty. If the superior to whom the vow is taken knows his business, he will quickly detect which things are really displeasing to his pupil, and familiarize him with them.

Disobedience to the superior is a contest between these two wills in the inferior. The will expressed in his vow, which is the will linked to his highest will by the fact that he has taken it in order to develop that highest will, contends with the temporary will, which is based only on temporary considerations.

The Teacher should then seek gently and firmly to key up the pupil, little by little, until obedience follows command without reference to what that command may be; as Loyola wrote: "perinde ac cadaver."

No one has understood the Magical Will better than Loyola; in his system the individual was forgotten. The will of the General was instantly echoed by every member of the Order; hence the Society of Jesus became the most formidable of the religious organizations of the world.

That of the Old Man of the Mountains was perhaps the next best.

The defect in Loyola's system is that the General was not God, and that owing to various other considerations he was not even necessarily the best man in the Order.

To become General of the Order he must have willed to become General of the Order; and because of this he could be nothing more.

To return to the question of the development of the Will. It is always something to pluck up the weeds, but the flower itself needs tending. Having crushed all volitions in ourselves, and if necessary in others, which we find opposing our real Will, that Will itself will grow naturally with greater freedom. But it is not only necessary to purify the temple itself and consecrate it; invocations must be made. Hence it is necessary to be constantly doing things of a positive, not merely of a negative nature, to affirm that Will.

Renunciation and sacrifice are necessary, but they are comparatively easy. There are a hundred ways of missing, and only one of hitting. To avoid eating beef is easy; to eat nothing but pork is very difficult.

Levi recommends that at times the Magical Will itself should be cut off, on the same principle as one can always work better after a "complete change." Levi is doubtless right, but he must be understood as saying this "for the hardness of men's hearts." The turbine is more efficient than a reciprocating engine; and his counsel is only good for the beginner.

Ultimately the Magical Will so identifies itself with the man's whole being that it becomes unconscious, and is as constant a force as gravitation. One may even be surprised at one's own acts, and have to reason out their connection. But let it be understood that when the Will has thus really raised itself to the height of Destiny, the man is no more likely to do wrong than he is to float off into the air.

One may be asked whether there is not a conflict between this development of the Will and Ethics.

The answer is Yes.

In the Grand Grimoire we are told " to buy an egg without haggling "; and attainment, and the next step in the path of attainment, is that pearl of great price, which when a man hath found he straightway selleth all that he hath, and buyeth that pearl.

With many people custom and habit—of which ethics is but the social expression—are the things most difficult to give up: and it is a useful practice to break any habit just to get into the way of being free from that form of slavery. Hence we have practices for breaking up sleep, for putting our bodies into strained and unnatural positions, for doing difficult exercises of breathing—all these, apart from any special merit they may have in themselves for any particular purpose, have the main merit that the man forces himself to do them despite any conditions that may exist. Having conquered internal resistance one may conquer external resistance more easily.

In a steamboat the engine must first overcome its own inertia before it can attack the resistance of the water.

When the will has thus ceased to be intermittent, it becomes necessary to consider its size. Gravitation gives an acceleration of thirty-two feet per second on this planet, on the moon very much less. And a Will, however single and however constant, may still be of no particular use, because the circumstances which oppose it may be altogether too strong, or because it is for some reason unable to get into touch with them. It is useless to wish for the moon. If one does so, one must consider by what means that Will may be made effective.

48

And though a man may have a tremendous Will in one direction it need not always be sufficient to help him in another; it may even be stupid.

There is the story of the man who practised for forty years to walk across the Ganges; and, having succeeded, was reproached by his Holy Guru, who said: "You are a great fool. All your neighbours have been crossing every day on a raft for two pice."

This occurs to most, perhaps to all, of us in our careers. We spend infinite pains to learn something, to achieve something, which when gained does not seem worth even the utterance of the wish.

But this is a wrong view to take. The discipline necessary in order to learn Latin will stand us in good stead when we wish to do something quite different.

At school our masters punished us; when we leave school, if we have not learned to punish ourselves, we have learned nothing.

In fact the only danger is that we may value the achievement in itself. The boy who prides himself on his school knowledge is in danger of becoming a college professor.

So the Guru of the water-walking Hindu only meant that it was now time to be dissatisfied with what he had done—and to employ his powers to some better end.

And, incidentally, since the divine Will is one, it will be found that there is no capacity which is not necessarily subservient to the destiny of the man who possesses it.

One may be unable to tell when a thread of a particular colour will be woven into the carpet of Destiny. It is only when the carpet is finished and seen from a proper distance that the position of that particular strand is seen to be necessary. From this one is tempted to break a lance on that most ancient battlefield, free-will and destiny.

But even though every man is "determined" so that every action is merely the passive resultant of the sum-total of the forces which have acted upon him from eternity, so that his own Will is only the echo of the Will of the Universe, yet that consciousness of "free-will" is valuable; and if he really understands it as being the partial and individual expression of that internal motion in a Universe whose sum is rest, by so much will he feel that harmony, that totality. And though the happiness which he experiences may be criticised as only one scale of a balance in whose other scale is an equal misery, there are those who hold that misery consists only in the feeling of separation from the Universe, and that consequently all may cancel out among the lesser feelings, leaving only that infinite bliss which is one phase of the infinite consciousness of that ALL. Such speculations are somewhat beyond the scope of the present remarks. It is of no particular moment to observe that the elephant and flea can be no other than they are; but

E

we do perceive that one is bigger than the other. That is the fact of practical importance.

We do know that persons can be trained to do things which they could not do without training—and anyone who remarks that you cannot train a person unless it is his destiny to be trained is quite unpractical. Equally it is the destiny of the trainer to train. There is a fallacy in the determinist argument similar to the fallacy which is the root of all "systems" of gambling at Roulette. The odds are just over three to one against red coming up twice running; but after red has come up once the conditions are changed.

It would be useless to insist on such a point were it not for the fact that many people confuse Philosophy with Magick. Philosophy is the enemy of Magick. Philosophy assures us that after all nothing matters, and that *che sarà sarà*.

In practical life, and Magick is the most practical of the Arts of life, this difficulty does not occur. It is useless to argue with a man who is running to catch a train that he may be destined not to catch it; he just runs, and if he could spare breath would say " Blow destiny! "

It has been said earlier that the real Magical Will must be toward the highest attainment, and this can never be until the flowering of the Magical Understanding. The Wand must be made to grow in length as well as in strength; it need not do so of its own nature.

The ambition of every boy is to be an engine-driver. Some attain it, and remain there all their lives.

But in the majority of cases the Understanding grows faster than the Will, and long before the boy is in a position to attain his wish he has already forgotten it.

In other cases the Understanding never grows beyond a certain point, and the Will persists without intelligence.

The business man (for example) has wished for ease and comfort, and to this end goes daily to his office and slaves under a more cruel taskmaster than the meanest of the workmen in his pay; he decides to retire, and finds that life is empty. The end has been swallowed up in the means.

Only those are happy who have desired the unattainable.

All possessions, the material and the spiritual alike, are but dust.

Love, sorrow, and compassion are three sisters who, if they seem freed from this curse, are only so because of their relation to The Unsatisfied.

Beauty is itself so unattainable that it escapes altogether; and the true artist, like the true mystic, can never rest. To him the Magician is but a servant. His wand is of infinite length; it is the creative Mahalingam.

The difficulty with such an one is naturally that his wand being very thin in proportion to its length is liable to wobble. Very few artists are conscious of their real purpose, and in very many cases we have this in-finite yearning supported by so frail a constitution that nothing is achieved.

The Magician must build all that he has into his pyramid; and if that pyramid is to touch the stars, how broad must be the base! There is no knowledge and no power which is useless to the Magician. One might almost say there is no scrap of material in the whole Universe with which he can dispense. His ultimate enemy is the great Magician, the Magician who created the whole illusion of the Universe; and to meet him in battle, so that nothing is left either of him or of yourself, you must be exactly equal to him.

At the same time let the Magician never forget that every brick must tend to the summit of the pyramid—the sides must be perfectly smooth; there must be no false summits, even in the lowest layers.

This is the practical and active form of that obligation of a Master of the Temple in which it is said: " I will interpret every phenomenon as a particular dealing of God with my soul."

In Liber CLXXV many practical devices for attaining this one-pointedness are given, and though the subject of that book is devotion to a particular Deity, its instructions may be easily generalized to suit the development of any form of will.

This will is then the active form of understanding. The Master of the Temple asks, on seeing a slug: "What is the purpose of this message from the Unseen? How shall I interpret this Word of God Most High?" The Magus thinks: "How shall I use this slug?" And in this course he must persist. Though many things useless, so far as he can see, are sent to him, one day he will find the one thing he needs, while his Understanding will appreciate the fact that none of those other things were useless.

So with these early practices of renunciation it will now be clearly understood that they were but of temporary use. They were only of value as training. The adept will laugh over his early absurdities—the disproportions will have been harmonized; and the structure of his soul will be seen as perfectly organic, with no one thing out of its place. He will see himself as the positive Tau with its ten complete squares within the triangle of the negatives; and this figure will become one, as soon as from the equilibrium of opposites he has attained to the identity of opposites.

In all this it will have been seen that **the most powerful weapon in the hand of the student is the Vow of Holy Obedience**; and many will wish that they had the opportunity of putting themselves under a holy Guru. Let them take heart—for any being capable of giving commands is an efficient Guru for the purpose of this Vow, provided that he is not too amiable and lazy.

The only reason for choosing a Guru who has himself attained is that he will aid the vigilance of the sleepy Chela, and, while tempering the Wind to that shorn lamb, will carefully harden him, and at the same time gladden his ears with holy discourse. But if such a person is inaccessible, let him choose any one with whom he has constant intercourse, explain the circumstances, and ask him to act.

The person should if possible be trustworthy; and let the Chela remember that if he should be ordered to jump over a cliff it is very much better to do it than to give up the practice.

And it is of the very greatest importance not to limit the vow in any way. You must buy the egg without haggling.

In a certain Society the members were bound to do certain things, being assured that there was "nothing in the vow contrary to their civil, moral, or religious obligations." So when any one wanted to break his vow he had no difficulty in discovering a very good reason for it. The vow lost all its force.

When Buddha took his seat under the blessed Bo-Tree, he took an oath that none of the inhabitants of the 10,000 worlds should cause him to rise until he had attained; so that when even Mara the great Arch-Devil, with his three daughters the arch-temptresses appeared, he remained still.

Now it is useless for the beginner to take so formidable a vow; he has not yet attained the strength which can defy Mara. Let him estimate his strength, and take a vow which is within it, but only just within it. Thus Milo began by carrying a new-born calf; and day by day as it grew into a bull, his strength was found sufficient.

Again let it be said that **Liber III is a most admirable method for the** beginner,[1] and it will be best, even if he is very confident in his strength, to take the vow for very short periods, beginning with an hour and increasing daily by half-hours until the day is filled. Then let him rest awhile, and attempt a two-day practice; and so on until he is perfect.

He should also begin with the very easiest practices. But the thing which he is sworn to avoid should not be a thing which normally he would do infrequently; because the strain on the memory which subserves his vigilance would be very great, and the practice become difficult. It is just as well at first that the pain of his arm should be

---

[1] This book must be carefully read. Its essence is that the pupil swears to refrain from a certain thought, word, or deed; and on each breach of the oath, cuts his arm sharply with a razor. This is better than flagellation because it can be done in public, without attracting notice. It however forms one of the most hilariously exciting parlour games for the family circle ever invented. Friends and relations are always ready to do their utmost to trap you into doing the forbidden thing.

there *at the time when he would normally do the forbidden thing,* to warn him against its repetition.

There will thus be a clear connection in his mind of cause and effect, until he will be just as careful in avoiding this particular act which he has consciously determined, as in those other things which in childhood he has been trained to avoid.

Just as the eyelid unconsciously closes when the eye is threatened,[1] so must he build up in consciousness this power of inhibition until it sinks below consciousness, adding to his store of automatic force, so that he is free to devote his conscious energy to a yet higher task.

It is impossible to overrate the value of this inhibition to the man when he comes to meditate. He has guarded his mind against thoughts A, B, and C; he has told the sentries to allow no one to pass who is not in uniform. And it will be very easy for him to extend that power, and to lower the portcullis.

Let him remember, too, that there is a difference not only in the frequency of thoughts—but in their intensity.

The worst of all is of course the ego, which is almost omnipresent

[1] If it were not so there would be very few people in the world who were not blind.

and almost irresistible, although so deeply-seated that in normal thought one may not always be aware of it.

Buddha, taking the bull by the horns, made this idea the first to be attacked.

Each must decide for himself whether this is a wise course to pursue. But it certainly seems easier to strip off first the things which can easily be done without.

The majority of people will find most trouble with the Emotions, and thoughts which excite them.

But it is both possible and necessary not merely to suppress the emotions, but to turn them into faithful servants. Thus the emotion of anger is occasionally useful against that portion of the brain whose slackness vitiates the control.

If there is one emotion which is never useful, it is pride; for this reason, that it is bound up entirely with the Ego . .

No, there is no use for pride !

The destruction of the Perceptions, either the grosser or the subtler, appears much easier, because the mind, not being moved, is free to remember its control.

It is easy to be so absorbed in a book that one takes no notice of the most beautiful scenery. But if stung by a wasp the book is immediately forgotten.

The Tendencies are, however, much harder to combat than the three lower Skandhas put together—for the simple reason that they are for the most part below consciousness, and must be, as it were, awakened in order to be destroyed, so that the will of the Magician is in a sense trying to do two opposite things at the same time.

Consciousness itself is only destroyed by Samadhi.

One can now see the logical process which begins in refusing to think of a foot, and ends by destroying the sense of individuality.

Of the methods of destroying various deep-rooted ideas there are many.

The best is perhaps the method of equilibrium. Get the mind into the habit of calling up the opposite to every thought that may arise. In conversation always disagree. See the other man's arguments; but, however much your judgment approves them, find the answer.

Let this be done dispassionately; the more convinced you are that a certain point of view is right, the more determined you should be to find proofs that it is wrong.

If you have done this thoroughly, these points of view will cease to trouble you; you can then assert your own point of view with the calm of a master, which is more convincing than the enthusiasm of a learner.

You will cease to be interested in controversies; politics, ethics, religion will seem so many toys, and your Magical Will will be free from these inhibitions.

In Burma there is only one animal which the people will kill, Russell's Viper; because, as they say, "either you must kill it or it will kill you"; and it is a question of which sees the other first.

Now any one idea which is not The Idea must be treated in this fashion. When you have killed the snake you can use its skin, but as long as it is alive and free, you are in danger.

And unfortunately the ego-idea, which is the real snake, can throw itself into a multitude of forms, each clothed in the most brilliant dress. Thus the devil is said to be able to disguise himself as an angel of light.

Under the strain of a magical vow this is too terribly the case. No normal human being understands or can understand the temptations of the saints.

An ordinary person with ideas like those which obsessed St. Patrick and St. Antony would be only fit for an asylum.

The tighter you hold the snake (which was previously asleep in the sun, and harmless enough, to all appearance), the more it struggles; and it is important to remember that your hold must tighten correspondingly, or it will escape and bite you.

Just as if you tell a child not to do a thing—no matter what—it will immediately want to do it, though otherwise the idea might never have entered its head, so it is with the saint. **We have all of us these tendencies latent in us;** of most of them we might remain unconscious all our lives—unless they were awakened by our Magick. They lie in ambush. **And every one must be awakened, and every one must be destroyed.** Every one who signs the oath of a Probationer is stirring up a hornets' nest.

A man has only to affirm his conscious aspiration; and the enemy is upon him.

It seems hardly possible that any one can ever pass through that terrible year of probation—and yet the aspirant is not bound to anything difficult; it almost seems as if he were not bound to anything at all—and yet experience teaches us that the effect is like plucking a man from his fireside into mid-Atlantic in a gale. The truth is, it may be, that the very simplicity of the task makes it difficult.

The Probationer must cling to his aspiration—affirm it again and again in desperation.

He has, perhaps, almost lost sight of it; it has become meaningless to him; he repeats it mechanically as he is tossed from wave to wave.

But if he can stick to it he will come through.

And, once he *is* through, things will again assume their proper aspect;

he will see that mere illusion were the things that seemed so real, and he will be fortified against the new trials that await him.

But unfortunate indeed is he who cannot thus endure. It is useless for him to say, "I don't like the Atlantic; I will go back to the fireside."

Once take one step on the path, and there is no return. You will remember in Browning's "Childe Roland to the dark Tower came"·

> For mark! no sooner was I fairly found
> Pledged to the plain, after a pace or two,
>   Than, pausing to throw backwards a last view
> O'er the safe road, 'twas gone: grey plain all round,
>   Nothing but plain to the horizon's bound.
> I might go on; naught else remained to do.

And this is universally true. The statement that the Probationer can resign when he chooses is in truth only for those who have taken the oath but superficially.

A real Magical Oath cannot be broken: you think it can, but it can't.

This is the advantage of a real Magical Oath.

However far you go around, you arrive at the end just the same, and all you have done by attempting to break your oath is to involve yourself in the most frightful trouble.

It cannot be too clearly understood that such is the nature of things: it does not depend upon the will of any persons, however powerful or exalted; nor can Their force, the force of Their great oaths, avail against the weakest oath of the most trivial of beginners.

The attempt to interfere with the Magical Will of another person would be wicked, if it were not absurd.

One may attempt to build up a Will when before nothing existed but a chaos of whims; but once organization has taken place it is sacred. As Blake says: "Everything that lives is holy"; and hence the creation of life is the most sacred of tasks. It does not matter very much to the creator what it is that he creates; there is room in the universe for both the spider and the fly.

It is from the rubbish-heap of Choronzon that one selects the material for a god!

This is the ultimate analysis of the Mystery of Redemption, and is possibly the real reason of the existence (if existence it can be called) of form, or, if you like, of the Ego.

It is astonishing that this typical cry—"I am I"—is the cry of that which above all is not I.

It was that Master whose Will was so powerful that at its lightest expression the deaf heard, and the dumb spake, lepers were cleansed and the dead arose to life, that Master and no other who at the supreme moment of his agony could cry, "Not my Will, but Thine, be done."

THE CUP

CHAPTER VII

AS the Magick Wand is the Will, the Wisdom, the Word of the Magician, so is the Magick Cup his Understanding.

This is the cup of which it was written: " Father, if it be Thy Will, let this cup pass from Me!" And again: " Can ye drink of the cup that I drink of?"

And it is also the cup in the hand of OUR LADY BABALON, and the cup of the Sacrament.

This Cup is full of bitterness, and of blood, and of intoxication.

The Understanding of the Magus is his link with the Invisible, on the passive side.

His Will errs actively by opposing itself to the Universal Will.

His Understanding errs passively when it receives influence from that which is not the ultimate truth.

In the beginning the Cup of the student is almost empty; and even such truth as he receives may leak away, and be lost.

They say that the Venetians made glasses which changed colour if poison was put into them; of such a glass must the student make his Cup.

Very little experience on the mystic path will show him that of all the impressions he receives none is true. Either they are false in themselves, or they are wrongly interpreted in his mind.

There is one truth, and only one. All other thoughts are false.

And as he advances in the knowledge of his mind he will come to understand that its whole structure is so faulty that it is quite incapable, even in its most exalted moods, of truth.

He will recognize that any thought merely establishes a relation between the Ego and the non-Ego.

Kant has shown that even the laws of nature are but the conditions of thought. And as the current of thought is the blood of the mind, it is said that the Magick Cup is filled with the blood of the Saints. **All thought must be offered up as a sacrifice.**

The Cup can hardly be described as a weapon. It is round like the pantacle—not straight like the wand and the dagger. Reception, not projection, is its nature.[1]

[1] As the Magician is in the position of God towards the Spirit that he evokes, he

So that which is round is to him a symbol of the influence from the higher. This circle symbolizes the Infinite, as every cross or Tau represents the Finite. That which is four square shows the Finite fixed into itself; for this reason the altar is foursquare. It is the solid basis from which all the operation proceeds. One form[1] of magical cup has a sphere beneath the bowl, and is supported upon a conical base.

This cup (crescent, sphere, cone) represents the three principles of the Moon, the Sun, and Fire, the three principles which, according to the Hindus, have course in the body.[2]

This is the Cup of Purification; as Zoroaster says:

"So therefore first the priest who governeth the works of fire must sprinkle with the lustral water of the loud-resounding sea."

It is the sea that purifies the world. And the "Great Sea" is in the Qabalah a name of Binah, "Understanding."

stands in the Circle, and the spirit in the Triangle; so the Magician is in the Triangle with respect to his own God.

[1] An ugly form. A better is given in the illustration.

[2] These "principles" are seen by the pupil when first he succeeds in stilling his mind. That one which happens to be in course at the moment is the one seen by him. This is so marvellous an experience, even for one who has pushed astral visions to a very high point, that he may mistake them for the End. See chapter on Dhyana.

The Hebrew letters corresponding to these principles are Gimel, Resh, and Shin, and the word formed by them means "a flower" and also "expelled," "cast forth."

It is by the Understanding of the Magus that his work is purified.

Binah, moreover, is the Moon, and the bowl of this cup is shaped like the moon.

This moon is the path of Gimel through which the influence from the Crown descends upon the Sun of Tiphereth.

And this is based upon the pyramid of fire which symbolizes the aspiration of the student.

In Hindu symbolism the Amrita or "dew of immortality"[1] drips constantly upon a man, but is burnt up by the gross fire of his appetites. Yogis attempt to catch and so preserve this dew by turning back the tongue in the mouth.

Concerning the water in this Cup, it may be said that just as the wand should be perfectly rigid, the ideal solid, so should the water be the ideal fluid.

The Wand is erect, and must extend to Infinity.

The surface of the water is flat, and must extend to Infinity.

One is the line, the other the plane.

But as the Wand is weak without breadth, so is the water false without depth. The Understanding of the Magus must include all things, and that understanding must be infinitely profound.

---

[1] A—, the privative particle; *mrita*, mortal.

H. G. Wells has said that "every word of which a man is ignorant represents an idea of which he is ignorant." And it is impossible perfectly to understand all things unless all things be first known.

Understanding is the structuralization of knowledge.

All impressions are disconnected, as the Babe of the Abyss is so terribly aware; and the Master of the Temple must sit for 106 seasons in the City of the Pyramids because this coördination is a tremendous task.

There is nothing particularly occult in this doctrine concerning knowledge and understanding.

A looking-glass receives all impressions but coördinates none.

The savage has none but the most simple associations of ideas.

Even the ordinary civilized man goes very little further.

All advance in thought is made by collecting the greatest possible number of facts, classifying them, and grouping them.

The philologist, though perhaps he only speaks one language, has a much higher type of mind than the linguist who speaks twenty.

This Tree of Thought is exactly paralleled by the tree of nervous structure.

Very many people go about nowadays who are exceedingly "well-informed," but who have not the slightest idea of the meaning of the facts they know. They have not developed the necessary higher part of the brain. Induction is impossible to them.

This capacity for storing away facts is compatible with actual imbecility. Some imbeciles have been able to store their memories with more knowledge than perhaps any sane man could hope to acquire.

This is the great fault of modern education—a child is stuffed with facts, and no attempt is made to explain their connection and bearing. The result is that even the facts themselves are soon forgotten.

Any first-rate mind is insulted and irritated by such treatment, and any first-rate memory is in danger of being spoilt by it.

No two ideas have any real meaning until they are harmonized in a third, and the operation is only perfect when these ideas are contradictory. This is the essence of the Hegelian logic.

The Magick Cup, as was shown above, is also the flower. It is the lotus which opens to the sun, and which collects the dew.

This Lotus is in the hand of Isis the great Mother. It is a symbol similar to the Cup in the hand of OUR LADY BABALON.

There are also the Lotuses in the human body, according to the Hindu system of Physiology referred to in the chapter on Dharana.[1]

[1] These Lotuses are all situated in the spinal column, which has three channels, Sushumna in the middle, Ida and Pingala on either side (*cf.* the Tree of Life). The central channel is compressed at the base by Kundalini, the magical power, a sleeping serpent. Awake her: she darts up the spine, and the Prana flows through the Sushumna. See " Raja-Yoga " for more details.

There is the lotus of three petals in the Sacrum, in which the Kundalini lies asleep. This lotus is the receptacle of reproductive force.

There is also the six-petalled lotus opposite the navel—which receives the forces which nourish the body.

There is also a lotus in the Solar plexus which receives the nervous forces.

The six-petalled lotus in the heart corresponds to Tiphereth, and receives those vital forces which are connected with the blood.

The sixteen-petalled lotus opposite the larynx receives the nourishment needed by the breath.

The two-petalled lotus of the pineal gland receives the nourishment needed by thought, while above the junction of the cranial structures is that sublime lotus, of a thousand and one petals, which receives the influence from on high; and in which, in the Adept, the awakened Kundalini takes her pleasure with the Lord of All.

All these lotuses are figured by the Magick Cup.

In man they are but partly opened, or only opened to their natural nourishment. In fact it is better to think of them as closed, as secreting that nourishment, which, because of the lack of sun, turns to poison.

The Magick Cup must have no lid, yet it must be kept veiled most carefully at all times, except when invocation of the Highest is being made.

This Cup must also be hidden from the profane. The Wand must be kept secret lest the profane, fearing it, should succeed in breaking it; the Cup lest, wishing to touch it, they should defile it.

Yet the sprinkling of its water not only purifies the Temple, but blesseth them that are without: freely must it be poured! But let no one know your real purpose, and let no one know the secret of your strength. Remember Samson! Remember Guy Fawkes!

Of the methods of increasing Understanding those of the Holy Qabalah are perhaps the best, provided that the intellect is thoroughly awake to their absurdity, and never allows itself to be convinced.[1]

Further meditation of certain sorts is useful: not the strict meditation which endeavours to still the mind, but such a meditation as Sammasati.[2]

On the exoteric side if necessary the mind should be trained by the study of any well-developed science, such as chemistry, or mathematics.

The idea of organization is the first step, that of interpretation the second. The Master of the Temple, whose grade corresponds to Binah, is sworn to "interpret every phenomenon as a particular dealing of God with his soul."

[1] See the "Interlude" following.
[2] See Equinox V, "The Training of the Mind"; Equinox II, "The Psychology of Hashish"; Equinox VII, "Liber DCCCCXIII."

But even the beginner may attempt this practice with advantage.

Either a fact fits in or it does not; if it does not, harmony is broken; and as the Universal harmony cannot be broken, the discord must be in the mind of the student, thus showing that he is not in tune with that Universal choir.

Let him then puzzle out first the great facts, then the little; until one summer, when he is bald and lethargic after lunch, he understands and appreciates the existence of flies!

This lack of Understanding with which we all begin is so terrible, so pitiful. In this world there is so much cruelty, so much waste, so much stupidity.

The contemplation of the Universe must be at first almost pure anguish. It is this fact which is responsible for most of the speculations of philosophy.

Mediaeval philosophers went hopelessly astray because their theology necessitated the reference of all things to the standard of men's welfare.

They even became stupid: Bernardin de St. Pierre (was it not?) said that the goodness of God was such that wherever men had built a great city, He had placed a river to assist them in conveying merchandise. But the truth is that in no way can we imagine the Universe as devised. If horses were made for men to ride, were not men made for worms to eat?

And so we find once more that **the Ego-idea must be ruthlessly rooted out before Understanding can be attained.**

There is an apparent contradiction between this attitude and that of the Master of the Temple. What can possibly be more selfish than this interpretation of everything as the dealing of God with the soul?

But it is God who is all and not any part; and every "dealing" must thus be an expansion of the soul, a destruction of its separateness.

Every ray of the sun expands the flower.

The surface of the water in the Magick Cup is infinite; there is no point different from any other point.[1]

Thus, ultimately, as the wand is a binding and a limitation, so is the Cup an expansion—into the Infinite.

And this is the danger of the Cup; it must necessarily be open to all, and yet if anything is put into it which is out of proportion, unbalanced or impure, it takes hurt.

And here again we find difficulty with our thoughts. The grossness and stupidity of *simple impressions* cloud the water; *emotions* trouble it; *perceptions* are still far from the perfect purity of truth; they cause re-

---

[1] "If ye confound the space-marks, saying: They are one, or saying: They are many . . . then expect the direful judgments of Ra Hoor Khuit. . . . This shall regenerate the world, the little world my sister." These are the words of NUIT, Our Lady of the Stars, of whom Binah is but the troubled reflection.

flections; while the *tendencies* alter the refractive index, and break up the light. Even *consciousness* itself is that which distinguishes between the lower and the higher, the waters which are below the firmament from the waters which are above the firmament, that appalling stage in the great curse of creation.

Since at the best this water [1] is but a reflection, how tremendously important it becomes that it should be still!

If the cup is shaken the light will be broken up.

Therefore the Cup is placed upon the Altar, which is foursquare, will multiplied by will, the confirmation of the will in the Magical Oath, its fixation in Law.

---

[1] The water in this Cup (the latter is also a heart, as shown by the transition from the ancient to the modern Tarot; the suit "Hearts" in old packs of cards, and even in modern Spanish and Italian cards, is called "Cups") is the letter *Mem* (the Hebrew word for water), which has for its Tarot trump the Hanged Man. This Hanged Man represents the Adept hanging by one heel from a gallows, which is in the shape of the letter Daleth—the letter of the Empress, the heavenly Venus in the Tarot. His legs form a cross, his arms a triangle, as if by his equilibrium and self-sacrifice he were bringing the light down and establishing it even in the abyss.

Elementary as this is, it is a very satisfactory hieroglyph of the Great Work, though the student is warned that the obvious sentimental interpretation will have to be discarded as soon as it has been understood. It is a very noble illusion, and therefore a very dangerous one, to figure one's self as the Redeemer. For, of all the illusions in this Cup—the subtler and purer they are, the more difficult they are to detect.

It is easy to see when water is muddy, and easy to get rid of the mud; but there are many impurities which defy everything but distillation and even some which must be fractionated unto 70 times 7.

There is, however, a universal solvent and harmonizer, a certain dew which is so pure that a single drop of it cast into the water of the Cup will for the time being bring all to perfection.

This dew is called Love. Even as in the case of human love, the whole Universe appears perfect to the man who is under its control, so is it, and much more, with the Divine Love of which it is now spoken.

For human love is an excitement, and not a stilling, of the mind; and as it is bound to the individual, only leads to greater trouble in the end.

This Divine Love, on the contrary, is attached to no symbol.

It abhors limitation, either in its intensity or its scope. And this is the dew of the stars of which it is spoken in the Holy Books, for NUIT the Lady of the Stars is called "the Continuous One of Heaven," and it is that Dew which bathes the body of the Adept "in a sweet-smelling perfume of sweat." [1]

In this cup, therefore, though all things are placed, by virtue of this

[1] See Liber Legis. Equinox VII.

dew all lose their identity. And therefore this Cup is in the hand of BABALON, the Lady of the City of the Pyramids, wherein no one can be distinguished from any other, wherein no one may sit until he has lost his name.

Of that which is in the Cup it is also said that it is wine. This is the Cup of Intoxication. Intoxication means poisoning, and in particular refers to the poison in which arrows are dipped (Greek τόξον, " a bow "). Think of the Vision of the Arrow in Liber 418, and look at the passages in the Holy Books which speak of the action of the spirit under the figure of a deadly poison.

For to each individual thing attainment means first and foremost the destruction of the individuality.

Each of our ideas must be made to give up the Self to the Beloved, so that we may eventually give up the Self to the Beloved in our turn.

It will be remembered in the History Lection [1] how the Adepts "who had with smiling faces abandoned their homes and their possessions— could with steady calm and firm correctness abandon the Great Work itself; for this is the last and greatest projection of the Alchemist."

The Master of the Temple has crossed the Abyss, has entered the Palace of the King's Daughter; he has only to utter one word, and all

[1] Liber LXI, the book given to those who wish to become Probationers of A∴ A∴.

is dissolved. But, instead of that, he is found hidden in the earth, tending a garden.

This mystery is all too complex to be elucidated in these fragments of impure thought; it is a suitable subject for meditation.

AN INTERLUDE

AN INTERLUDE[1]

EVERY nursery rime contains profound magical secrets which are open to every one who has made a study of the correspondences of the Holy Qabalah. To puzzle out an imaginary meaning for this "nonsense" sets one thinking of the Mysteries; one enters into deep contemplation of holy things, and God Himself leads the soul to a real illumination. Hence also the necessity of Incarnation: the soul must descend into all falsity in order to attain All-Truth.

For instance:

> Old Mother Hubbard
> Went to her cupboard
> To get her poor dog a bone;
> When she got there,

---

[1] This chapter was dictated in answer to a casual remark by Soror Virakam. Fra. P. said jokingly that everything contained the Truth, if you knew how to find it; and, being challenged, proceeded to make good. It is here inserted, not for any value that it may have, but to test the reader. If it is thought to be a joke, the reader is one useless kind of fool; if it is thought that Fra. P. believes that the makers of the rimes had any occult intention, he is another useless kind of fool. Soror Virakam chose the rimes at hazard.

The cupboard was bare,
And so the poor dog had none.

Who is this ancient and venerable mother of whom it is spoken? Verily she is none other than Binah, as is evident in the use of the holy letter H with which her name begins.

Nor is she the sterile Mother Ama—but the fertile Aima; for within her she bears Vau, the son, for the second letter of her name, and R, the penultimate, is the Sun, Tiphereth, the Son.

The other three letters of her name, B, A, and D, are the three paths which join the three supernals.

To what cupboard did she go? Even to the most secret caverns of the Universe. And who is this dog? Is it not the name of God spelt Qabalistically backwards? And what is this bone? This bone is the Wand, the holy Lingam!

The complete interpretation of the rune is now open. This rime is the legend of the murder of Osiris by Typhon.

The limbs of Osiris were scattered in the Nile.

Isis sought them in every corner of the Universe, and she found all except his sacred lingam, which was not found until quite recently (*vide* Fuller, "The Star in the West").

Let us take another example from this rich storehouse of magick lore.

> Little Bo Peep,
> She lost her sheep,
> And couldn't tell where to find them.
> Leave them alone!
> And they'll come home,
> Dragging their tails behind them.

" Bo " is the root meaning Light, from which spring such words as Bo-tree, Bodhisattva, and Buddha.

And " Peep " is Apep, the serpent Apophis. This poem therefore contains the same symbol as that in the Egyptian and Hebrew Bibles.

The snake is the serpent of initiation, as the Lamb is the Saviour.

This ancient one, the Wisdom of Eternity, sits in its old anguish awaiting the Redeemer. And this holy verse triumphantly assures us that there is no need for anxiety. The Saviours will come one after the other, at their own good pleasure, and as they may be needed, and drag their tails, that is to say those who follow out their holy commandment, to the ultimate goal.

Again we read:

> Little Miss Muffett
> Sat on a tuffet,
> Eating of curds and whey,
> Up came a big spider,
> And sat down beside her,
> And frightened Miss Muffett away.

Little Miss Muffett unquestionably represents Malkah; for she is unmarried. She is seated upon a "tuffet"; *id est*, she is the unregencrate soul upon Tophet, the pit of hell. And she eats curds and whey, that is, not the pure milk of the mother, but milk which has undergone decomposition.

But who is the spider? Verily herein is a venerable arcanum connoted! Like all insects, the spider represents a demon. But why a spider? Who is this spider "who taketh hold with her hands, and is in King's Palaces"? The name of this spider is Death. It is the fear of death which first makes the soul aware of its forlorn condition.

It would be interesting if tradition had preserved for us Miss Muffett's subsequent adventures.

But we must proceed to consider the interpretation of the following rime:

> Little Jack Horner
> Sat in a corner,
> Eating a Christmas pie.
> He stuck in his thumb,
> And pulled out a plum,
> And said: "What a good boy am I!"

In the interpretation of this remarkable poem there is a difference between two great schools of Adepts.

One holds that Jack is merely a corruption of John, Ion, he who goes

—Hermes, the Messenger. The other prefers to take Jack simply and reverently as Iacchus, the spiritual form of Bacchus. But it does not matter very much whether we insist upon the swiftness or the rapture of the Holy Spirit of God; and that it is He of whom it is here spoken is evident, for the name Horner could be applied to none other by even the most casual reader of the Holy Gospels and the works of Congreve. And the context makes this even clearer, for he sits in a corner, that is in the place of Christ, the Corner Stone, eating, that is, enjoying, that which the birth of Christ assures to us. He is the Comforter who replaces the absent Saviour. If there was still any doubt of His identity it would be cleared up by the fact that it is the thumb, which is attributed to the element of Spirit, and not one of the four fingers of the four lesser elements, which he sticks into the pie of the new dispensation. He plucks forth one who is ripe, no doubt to send him forth as a teacher into the world, and rejoices that he is so well carrying out the will of the Father.

Let us pass from this most blessèd subject to yet another.

> Tom, Tom, the piper's son,
> Stole a pig and away he run.
> The pig was eat,
> And Tom was beat,
> And Tom went roaring down the street.

This is one of the more exoteric of these rimes. In fact, it is not much better than a sun-myth. Tom is Toum, the God of the Sunset (called the Son of Apollo, the Piper, the maker of music). The only difficulty in the poem concerns the pig; for anyone who has watched an angry sunset in the Tropics upon the sea, will recognize how incomparable a description of that sunset is given in that wonderful last line. Some have thought that the pig refers to the evening sacrifice, others that she is Hathor, the Lady of the West, in her more sensual aspect.

But it is probable that this poem is only the first stanza of an epic. It has all the characteristic marks. Someone said of the Iliad that it did not finish, but merely stopped. This is the same. We may be sure that there is more of this poem. It tells us too much and too little. How came this tragedy of the eating of a merely stolen pig? Unveil this mystery of who " eat " it!

It must be abandoned, then, as at least partially insoluble. Let us consider this poem:

> Hickory, dickory, dock!
> The mouse ran up the clock;
> The clock struck one,
> And the mouse ran down,
> Hickory, dickory, dock!

Here we are on higher ground at once. The clock symbolizes the spinal column, or, if you prefer it, Time, chosen as one of the conditions of normal consciousness. The mouse is the Ego; "*Mus*," a mouse, being only *Sum*, " I am," spelt Qabalistically backwards.

This Ego or Prana or Kundalini force being driven up the spine, the clock strikes one, that is, the duality of consciousness is abolished. And the force again subsides to its original level.

" Hickory, dickory, dock!" is perhaps merely the mantra which was used by the Adept who constructed this rime, thereby hoping to fix it in the minds of men, so that they might attain to Samadhi by the same method. Others attribute to it a more profound significance—which it is impossible to go into at this moment, for we must turn to:—

> Humpty Dumpty sat on the wall;
> Humpty Dumpty got a great fall;
> All the king's horses
> And all the king's men
> Couldn't set up Humpty Dumpty again.

This is so simple as hardly to require explanation. Humpty Dumpty is of course the Egg of Spirit, and the wall is the Abyss—his " fall " is therefore the descent of spirit into matter; and it is only too painfully familiar to us that all the king's horses and all his men cannot restore us to the height.

Only The King Himself can do that!

But one hardly dare comment upon a theme which has been so fruit-
fully treated by Ludovicus Carolus, that most holy illuminated man of
God. His masterly treatment of the identity of the three reciprocating
paths of Daleth, Teth, and Pe, is one of the most wonderful passages in
all the Holy Qabalah. His resolution of what we take to be the bond
of slavery into very love, the embroidered neckband of honour bestowed
upon us by the King himself, is one of the most sublime passages in this
class of literature.

> Peter, Peter, pumpkin eater,
> Had a wife and couldn't keep her.
> He put her in a peanut shell;
> Then he kept her very well.

This early authentic text of the Hinayana school of Buddhism is
much esteemed even to-day by the more cultured and devoted followers
of that school.

The pumpkin is of course the symbol of resurrection, as is familiar to
all students of the story of Jonah and the gourd.

Peter is therefore the Arahat who has put an end to his series of
resurrections. That he is called Peter is a reference to the symbolizing
of Arahats as stones in the great wall of the guardians of mankind. His
wife is of course (by the usual symbolism) his body, which he could not
keep until he put her in a peanut shell, the yellow robe of a Bhikkhu.

Buddha said that if any man became an Arahat he must either take the vows of a Bhikkhu that very day, or die, and it is this saying of Buddha's that the unknown poet wished to commemorate.

> Taffy was a Welshman,
> Taffy was a thief;
> Taffy came to my house
> And stole a leg of beef.
> I went to Taffy's house;
> Taffy was in bed.
> I took a carving knife,
> And cut off Taffy's head.

Taffy is merely short for Taphtatharath, the Spirit of Mercury and the God of Welshmen or thieves. " My house" is of course equivalent to " my magick circle." Note that Beth, the letter of Mercury and " The Magus," means "a house."

The beef is the symbol of the Bull, Apis the Redeemer. This is therefore that which is written: " Oh my God, disguise thy glory! Come as a thief, and let us steal away the sacraments!"

In the following verse we find that Taffy is "in bed," owing to the operation of the sacrament. The great task of the Alchemist has been accomplished; the mercury is fixed.

One can then take the Holy Dagger, and separate the Caput Mortuum from the Elixir. Some Alchemists believe that the beef represents that dense physical substance which is imbibed by Mercury for his fixation; but here as always we should prefer the more spiritual interpretation.

> Bye, Baby Bunting!
> Daddy's gone a-hunting.
> He's gone to get a rabbit-skin
> To wrap my Baby Bunting in.

This is a mystical charge to the new-born soul to keep still, to remain steadfast in meditation; for, in *Bye*, Beth is the letter of thought, Yod that of the Hermit. It tells the soul that the Father of All will clothe him about with His own majestical silence. For is not the rabbit he " who lay low and said nuffin' "?

> Pat-a-cake, pat-a-cake, baker's man!
> Bake me a cake as fast as you can!
> Pat it and prick it and mark it with P!
> Bake it in the oven for baby and me!

This rime is usually accompanied (even to-day in the nursery) with a ceremonial clapping of hands—the symbol of Samadhi. Compare what is said on this subject in our comment on the famous " Advent " passage in Thessalonians.

The cake is of course the bread of the sacrament, and it would ill become Frater P. to comment upon the third line—though it may be remarked that even among the Catholics the wafer has always been marked with a phallus or cross.

(Note by Soror Virakam.)

(Nearly midnight. At this moment we stopped dictating, and began to converse. Then Fra. P. said: "Oh, if I could only dictate a book like the Tao Teh King!" Then he closed his eyes as if meditating. Just before I had noticed a change in his face, most extraordinary, as if he were no longer the same person; in fact in the ten minutes we were talking he seemed to be any number of different people. I especially noticed the pupils of his eyes were so enlarged that the entire eye seemed black. (I tremble so and have such a quaking feeling inside, simply in thinking of last night, that I can't form letters.) Then quite slowly the entire room filled with a thick yellow light (deep golden, but not brilliant. I mean not dazzling, but soft). Fra. P. looked like a person I had never seen but seemed to know quite well—his face, clothes and all were of this same yellow. I was so disturbed that I looked up to the ceiling to see what caused the light, but could only see the candles. Then the chair on which he sat seemed to rise; it was like a throne, and he seemed to be either dead or sleeping, but it was certainly no longer Fra. P. This frightened me, and I tried to understand by looking round the room; when I looked back the chair was raised, and he was still the same. I realized I was alone; and thinking he was dead or gone—or some other terrible thing—I lost consciousness).

(This discourse has been thus left unfinished; but it is only necessary to add that the capacity to extract such spiritual honey from these unpromising flowers is the mark of an adept who has perfected his Magick Cup. This method of Qabalistic exegesis is one of the best ways of exalting the reason to the higher consciousness. Evidently it "started" Fra. P. so that in a moment he became completely concentrated and entranced.[1] Ed.)

[1] See remarks on absurdity of prayer in " Eleusis " (Crowley, "Collected Works," vol. iii, pp. 223, 224.

THE SWORD

CHAPTER VIII

THE SWORD

"THE word of the Lord is quick and powerful, and sharper than a two-edged sword."

As the Wand is Chokmah, the Will, "the Father," and the Cup the Understanding, "the Mother," Binah; so the Magick Sword is the Reason, "the Son," the six Sephiroth of the Ruach, and we shall see that the Pantacle corresponds to Malkuth, "the Daughter."

The Magick Sword is the analytical faculty; directed against any demon it attacks his complexity.

Only the simple can withstand the sword. As we are below the Abyss, this weapon is then entirely destructive: it divides Satan against Satan. It is only in the lower forms of Magick, the purely human forms, that the Sword has become so important a weapon. A dagger should be sufficient.

But the mind of man is normally so important to him that the sword is actually the largest of his weapons; happy is he who can make the dagger suffice!

The hilt of the Sword should be made of copper.

The guard is composed of the two crescents of the waxing and the waning moon—back to back. Spheres are placed between them, forming an equilateral triangle with the sphere of the pommel.

The blade is straight, pointed, and sharp right up to the guard. It is made of steel, to equilibrate with the hilt, for steel is the metal of Mars, as copper is of Venus.

Those two planets are male and female—and thus reflect the Wand and the Cup, though in a much lower sense.

The hilt is of Venus, for **Love is the motive of this ruthless analysis**—if this were not so the sword would be a Black Magical weapon.

The pommel of the Sword is in Death, the guard extends to Chesed and Geburah; the point is in Malkuth. Some magi make the three spheres of lead, tin, and gold respectively; the moons are silver, and the grip contains quicksilver, thus making the Sword symbolic of the seven planets. But this is a phantasy and affectation.

"Whoso taketh the sword shall perish by the sword," is not a mystical threat, but a mystical promise. It is our own complexity that must be destroyed.

Here is another parable. Peter, the Stone of the Philosophers, cuts off the ear of Malchus, the servant of the High Priest (the ear is the organ of Spirit). In analysis the spiritual part of Malkuth must be separated from it by the philosophical stone, and then Christus, the Anointed One, makes it whole once more. "Solve et coagula!"

It is noticeable that this takes place at the arrest of Christ, who is the son, the Ruach, immediately before his crucifixion.

The Calvary Cross should be of six squares, an unfolded cube, which cube is this same philosophical stone.

Meditation will reveal many mysteries which are concealed in this symbol.

The Sword or Dagger is attributed to air, all-wandering, all-penetrating, but unstable; not a phenomenon subtle like fire, not a chemical combination like water, but a mixture of gases.[1]

The Sword, necessary as it is to the Beginner, is but a crude weapon.

---

[1] The Oxygen in the air would be too fierce for life; it must be largely diluted with the inert nitrogen.

The rational mind supports life, but about seventy-nine per cent. of it not only refuses itself to enter into combination, but prevents the remaining twenty-one per cent. from doing so. Enthusiasms are checked; the intellect is the great enemy of devotion. One of the tasks of the Magician is to manage somehow to separate the Oxygen and Nitrogen in his mind, to stifle four-fifths so that he may burn up the remainder, a flame of holiness. But this cannot be done by the Sword.

Its function is to keep off the enemy or to force a passage through them—and though it must be wielded to gain admission to the palace, it cannot be worn at the marriage feast.

One might say that the Pantacle is the bread of life, and the Sword the knife which cuts it up. One must have ideas, but one must criticize them.

The Sword, too, is that weapon with which one strikes terror into the demons and dominates them. One must keep the Ego Lord of the impressions. One must not allow the circle to be broken by the demon; one must not allow any one idea to carry one away.

It will readily be seen how very elementary and false all this is—but for the beginner it is necessary.

In all dealings with demons the point of the Sword is kept downwards, and it should not be used for invocation, as is taught in certain schools of magick.

If the Sword is raised towards the Crown, it is no longer really a sword. The Crown cannot be divided. Certainly the Sword should not be lifted.

The Sword may, however, be clasped in both hands, and kept steady and erect, symbolizing that thought has become one with the single aspiration, and burnt up like a flame. This flame is the Shin, the Ruach Alhim, not the mere Ruach Adam. The divine and not the human consciousness.

The Magician cannot wield the Sword unless the Crown is on his head.

Those Magicians, who have attempted to make the Sword the sole or even the principal weapon, have only destroyed themselves, not by the destruction of combination, but by the destruction of division.[1] Weakness overcomes strength.

The most stable political edifice of history has been that of China, which was founded principally on politeness; and that of India has proved strong enough to absorb its many conquerors.[2]

The Sword has been the great weapon of the last century. Every idea has been attacked by thinkers, and none has withstood attack. Hence civilization crumbles.

No settled principles remain. To-day all constructive statesmanship is empiricism or opportunism. It has been doubted whether there is any real relation between Mother and Child, any real distinction between Male and Female.

The human mind, in despair, seeing insanity imminent in the breaking

[1] It should be noted that this ambiguity in the word "destruction" has been the cause of much misunderstanding. *Solve* is destruction, but so is *coagula*. The aim of the Magus is to destroy his partial thought by uniting it with the Universal Thought, not to make a further breach and division in the Whole.

[2] The Brahmin caste is not so strict as that of the "heaven-born" (Indian Civil Service).

up of these coherent images, has tried to replace them by ideals which are only saved from destruction, at the very moment of their birth, by their vagueness.

The Will of the King was at least ascertainable at any moment; nobody has yet devised a means for ascertaining the will of the people.

All conscious willed action is impeded; the march of events is now nothing but inertia.

Let the Magician consider these matters before he takes the Sword in his hand. Let him understand that the Ruach, this loose combination of 6 Sephiroth, only bound together by their attachment to the human will in Tiphereth, must be rent asunder.

The mind must be broken up into a form of insanity before it can be transcended.

David said: "I hate thoughts."

The Hindu says: "That which can be thought is not true."

Paul said: "The carnal mind is enmity against God."

And every one who meditates, even for an hour, will soon discover how this gusty aimless wind makes his flame flicker. "The wind bloweth where it listeth." The normal man is less than a straw.[1]

---

[1] But as it is said, *Similia similibus curantur*, we find this Ruach also the symbol of the Spirit. RVCh ALHIM, the Spirit of God, is 300, the number of the holy letter Shin. As this is the breath, which by its nature is double, the two edges of the

The connection between Breath and Mind has been supposed by some to exist merely in etymology. But the connection is a truer one.[1]

In any case there is undoubtedly a connection between the respiratory and mental functions. The Student will find this out by practising Pranayama. By this exercise some thoughts are barred, and those which do come into the mind come more slowly than before, so that the mind has time to perceive their falsity and to destroy them.

On the blade of the Magick Sword is etched the name AGLA, a Notariqon formed from the initials of the sentence *Ateh Gibor Leolahm Adonai*, "To Thee be the Power unto the Ages, O my Lord."

And the acid which eats into the steel should be oil of vitriol. Vitriol is a Notariqon of "Visita Interiora Terrae Rectificando Invenies Occultum Lapidem." That is to say: By investigating everything and

Sword, the letter H symbolises breath, and H is the letter of Aries—the House of Mars, of the Sword: and H is also the letter of the Mother; this is the link between the Sword and the Cup.

[1] It is undoubted that Ruach means primarily "that which moves or revolves," "a going," "a wheel," "the wind," and that its secondary meaning was mind because of the observed instability of mind, and its tendency to a circular motion. "Spiritus" only came to mean Spirit in the modern technical sense owing to the efforts of the theologians. We have an example of the proper use of the word in the term: Spirit of Wine—the airy portion of wine. But the word "inspire" was perhaps derived from observing the derangement of the breathing of persons in divine ecstasy.

bringing it into harmony and proportion you will find the hidden stone, the same stone of the philosophers of which mention has already been made, which turns all into gold. This oil which can eat into the steel, is further that which is written, Liber LXV, i, 16: "As an acid eats into steel   so am I unto the Spirit of Man."

Note how closely woven into itself is all this symbolism!

The centre of Ruach being the heart, it is seen that this Sword of the Ruach must be thrust by the Magician into his own heart.

But there is a subsequent task, of which it is spoken—Liber VII, v, 47. "He shall await the sword of the Beloved and bare his throat for the stroke." In the throat is Daath—the throne of Ruach. Daàth is Knowledge. This final destruction of knowledge opens the gate of the City of the Pyramids.

It is also written, Liber CCXX, iii, 11: "Let the woman be girt with a sword before me." But this refers to the arming of Vedana with Sañña, the overcoming of emotion by clarity of perception.

It is also spoken, Liber LXV, v, 14, of the Sword of Adonai, "that hath four blades, the blade of the Thunderbolt, the blade of the Pylon, the blade of the Serpent, the blade of the Phallus."

But this Sword is not for the ordinary Magician. For this is the Sword flaming every way that keeps Eden, and in this Sword the Wand and the Cup are concealed—so that although the being of the Magician is blasted by the Thunderbolt, and poisoned by the Serpent, at the same time the organs whose union is the supreme sacrament are left in him.

At the coming of Adonai the individual is destroyed in both senses. He is shattered into a thousand pieces, yet at the same time united with the simple.[1]

Of this it is also spoken by St. Paul in his Epistle to the Church in Thessalonica: "For the Lord shall descend from Heaven, with a shout, with the voice of the Archangel, and with the trump of God; and the dead in Christ shall rise first. Then we which are alive and remain shall be caught up together with them into the clouds to meet the Lord in the air; and so shall we be for ever with the Lord."

The stupid interpretation of this verse as prophetic of a "second advent" need not concern us; every word of it is, however, worthy of profound consideration.

"The Lord" is Adonai—which is the Hebrew for "my Lord"; and He descends from heaven, the supernal Eden, the Sahasrara Cakkra in man, with a "shout," a "voice," and a "trump," again airy symbols, for it is air that carries sound. These sounds refer to those heard by the Adept at the moment of rapture.

---

[1] Compare the first set of verses in Liber XVI. (XVI in the Taro is Pé, Mars, the Sword.)

This is most accurately pictured in the Tarot Trump called "The Angel," which corresponds to the letter Shin, the letter of Spirit and of Breath.

The whole mind of man is rent by the advent of Adonai, and is at once caught up into union with Him. "In the air," the Ruach.

Note that etymologically the word συν, "together with," is the Sanskrit *Sam*; and the Hebrew ADNI is the Sanskrit ADHI.

The phrase "together with the Lord," is then literally identical with the word Samadhi, which is the Sanskrit name of the phenomenon described by Saint Paul, this union of the ego and the non-ego, subject and object, this chymical marriage, and thus identical with the symbolism of the Rosy Cross, under a slightly different aspect.

And since marriage can only take place between one and one, it is evident that no idea can thus be united, unless it is simple.

Hence every idea must be analysed by the Sword. Hence, too, there must only be a single thought in the mind of the person meditating.

One may now go on to consider the use of the Sword in purifying emotions into perceptions.

It was the function of the Cup to interpret the perceptions by the tendencies; the Sword frees the perceptions from the Web of emotion.

The perceptions are meaningless in themselves; but the emotions are worse, for they delude their victim into supposing them significant and true.

Every emotion is an obsession; the most horrible of blasphemies is to attribute any emotion to God in the macrocosm, or to the pure soul in the microcosm.

How can that which is self-existent, complete, be *moved*? It is even written that "torsion about a point is iniquity."

But if the point itself could be moved it would cease to be itself, for position is the only attribute of the point.

The Magician must therefore make himself absolutely free in this respect.

It is the constant practice of Demons to attempt to terrify, to shock, to disgust, to allure. Against all this he must oppose the Steel of the Sword. If he has got rid of the ego-idea this task will be comparatively easy; unless he has done so it will be almost impossible. So says the Dhammapada:

> Me he abused, and me he beat, he robbed me, he insulted me:
> In whom such thoughts find harbourage, hatred will never cease to be.

And this hatred is the thought which inhibits the love whose apotheosis is Samadhi.

But it is too much to expect of the young Magician to practise attachment to the distasteful; let him first become indifferent. Let him endeavour to see facts as facts, as simply as he would see them if they were historical. Let him avoid the imaginative interpretation of any facts. Let him not put himself in the place of the people of whom the facts are related, or if he does so, let it be done only for the purpose of comprehension. Sympathy,[1] indignation, praise and blame, are out of place in the observer.

No one has properly considered the question as to the amount and quality of the light afforded by candles made by waxed Christians.

Who has any idea which joint of the ordinary missionary is preferred by epicures? It is only a matter of conjecture that Catholics are better eating than Presbyterians.

Yet these points and their kind are the only ones which have any importance at the time when the events occur.

Nero did not consider what unborn posterity might think of him; it is difficult to credit cannibals with the calculation that the recital of their exploits will induce pious old ladies to replenish their larder.

Very few people have ever *seen* a bull-fight. One set of people goes for excitement, another set for the perverse excitement which real or simulated horror affords. Very few people know that blood freshly

---

[1] It is true that sometimes sympathy is necessary to comprehension.

spilled in the sunlight is perhaps the most beautiful colour that is to be found in nature.

It is a notorious fact that it is practically impossible to get a reliable description of what occurs at a spiritualistic *séance*; the emotions cloud the vision.

Only in the absolute calm of the laboratory, where the observer is perfectly indifferent to what may happen, only concerned to observe exactly what that happening is, to measure and to weigh it by means of instruments incapable of emotion, can one even begin to hope for a truthful record of events. Even the common physical bases of emotion, the senses of pleasure and pain, lead the observer infallibly to err. This though they be not sufficiently excited to disturb his mind.

Plunge one hand into a basin of hot water, the other into a basin of cold water, then both together into a basin of tepid water; the one hand will say hot, the other cold.

Even in instruments themselves, their physical qualities, such as expansion and contraction (which may be called, in a way, the roots of pleasure and pain), cause error.

Make a thermometer, and the glass is so excited by the necessary fusion that year by year, for thirty years afterwards or more, the height of the mercury will continue to alter; how much more then with so plastic a matter as the mind! There is no emotion which does not leave a mark on the mind, and all marks are bad marks. Hope and fear are only opposite phases of a single emotion; both are incompatible with the purity of the soul. With the passions of man the case is somewhat different, as they are functions of his own will. They need to be disciplined, not to be suppressed. But emotion is impressed from without. It is an invasion of the circle.

As the Dhammapada says:

> An ill-thatched house is open to the mercy of the rain and wind;
> So passion hath the power to break into an unreflecting mind.
> A well-thatched house is proof against the fury of the rain and wind;
> So passion hath no power to break into a rightly-ordered mind.

Let then the Student practise observation of those things which normally would cause him emotion; and let him, having written a careful description of what he sees, check it by the aid of some person familiar with such sights.

Surgical operations and dancing girls are fruitful fields for the beginner.

In reading emotional books such as are inflicted on children let him always endeavour to see the event from the standpoint opposite to that of the author. Yet let him not emulate the partially emancipated child who complained of a picture of the Colosseum that "there was one poor little lion who hadn't got any Christian," except in the first instance. Adverse criticism is the first step; the second must go further.

Having sympathized sufficiently with both the lions and the Christians, let him open his eyes to that which his sympathy had masked thitherto, that the picture is abominably conceived, abominably composed, abominably drawn, and abominably coloured, as it is pretty sure to be.

Let him further study those masters, in science or in art, who have observed with minds untinctured by emotion.

Let him learn to detect idealizations, to criticize and correct them.

Let him understand the falsehood of Raphael, of Watteau, of Leighton, of Bouguereau; let him appreciate the truthfulness of John, of Rembrandt, of Titian, of O'Conor.

Similar studies in literature and philosophy will lead to similar results. But do not let him neglect the analysis of his own emotions; for until these are overcome he will be incapable of judging others.

This analysis may be carried out in various ways; one is the materialistic way. For example, if oppressed by nightmare, let him explain: " This nightmare is a cerebral congestion."

The strict way of doing this by meditation is Mahasatipatthana,[1] but

[1] See Crowley, " Collected Works," vol. ii, pp. 252-254.

it should be aided in every moment of life by endeavouring to estimate occurrences at their true value. Their relativity in particular must be carefully considered.

Your toothache does not hurt any one outside a very small circle. Floods in China mean to you nothing but a paragraph in the newspaper. The destruction of the world itself would have no significance in Sirius. One can hardly imagine even that the astronomers of Sirius could perceive so trifling a disturbance.

Now considering that Sirius itself is only, as far as you know, but one, and one of the least important, of the ideas in your mind, why should that mind be disturbed by your toothache? It is not possible to labour this point without tautology, for it is a very simple one; but it should be emphasised, for it is a very simple one. **Waugh! Waugh! Waugh! Waugh! Waugh!**[1]

In the question of ethics it again becomes vital for to many people it seems impossible to consider the merits of any act without dragging in a number of subjects which have no real connection with it.

The Bible has been mistranslated by perfectly competent scholars because they had to consider the current theology. The most glaring example is the "Song of Solomon," a typical piece of Oriental erotic-

[1] By interrupting thus doggishly, the bark of a dog will remind you, for the next week or two, of this.

ism. But since to admit that it was this would never do for a canonical book, they had to pretend that it was symbolical.

They tried to refine away the grossness of the expressions, but even their hardihood proved unequal to the task.

This form of dishonesty reaches its climax in the expurgating of the classics. "The Bible is the Word of God, written by holy men, as they were inspired by the Holy Ghost. But we will cut out those passages which we think unsuitable." "Shakespeare is our greatest poet—but, of course, he is very dreadful." "No one can surpass the lyrics of Shelley, but we must pretend that he was not an atheist."

Some translators could not bear that the heathen Chinese should use the word Shang Ti, and pretended that it did not mean God. Others, compelled to admit that it did mean God, explained that the use of the term showed that "God had not left himself without a witness even in this most idolatrous of nations. They had been mysteriously compelled to use it, not knowing what it meant." All this because of their emotional belief that they were better than the Chinese.

The most dazzling example of this is shown in the history of the study of Buddhism.

The early scholars simply could not understand that the Buddhist canon denies the soul, regards the ego as a delusion caused by a special faculty of the diseased mind, could not understand that the goal of the

Buddhist, Nibbana, was in any way different from their own goal, Heaven, in spite of the perfect plainness of the language in such dialogues as those between the Arahat Nagaśena and King Melinda ; and their attempts to square the text with their preconceptions will always stand as one of the great follies of the wise.

Again, it is almost impossible for the well-mannered Christian to realize that Jesus Christ ate with his fingers. The temperance advocate makes believe that the wine at the marriage feast of Cana was non-alcoholic.

It is a sort of mad syllogism.

Nobody whom I respect does this.

I respect So-and-so.

Therefore, So-and-so did not do this.

The moralist of to-day is furious when one points to the fact that practically every great man in history was grossly and notoriously immoral.

Enough of this painful subject!

As long as we try to fit facts to theories instead of adopting the scientific attitude of altering the theories (when necessary) to fit the facts, we shall remain mired in falsehood.

The religious taunt the scientific man with this open-mindedness, with this adaptability. "Tell a lie and stick to it!" is *their* golden rule.

There is no need to explain to even the humblest student of the magick of light to what this course of action tends.

Whether Genesis be true or geology be true, a geologist who believes in Genesis will go to Gehenna. " Ye cannot serve God and Mammon."

THE PANTACLE

THE SIGILLUM DEI ÆMETH, A PANTACLE
MADE BY DR. JOHN DEE.

CHAPTER IX

THE PANTACLE

AS the Magick Cup is the heavenly food of the Magus, so is the Magick Pantacle his earthly food.

The Wand was his divine force, and the Sword his human force.

The Cup is hollow to receive the influence from above. The Pantacle is flat like the fertile plains of earth.

The name Pantacle implies an image of the All, *omne in parvo*; but this is by a magical transformation of the Pantacle. Just as we made the Sword symbolical of everything by the force of our Magick, so do we work upon the Pantacle. That which is merely a piece of common bread shall be the body of God!

The Wand was the will of man, his wisdom, his word; the Cup was his understanding, the vehicle of grace; the Sword was his reason; and the Pantacle shall be his body, the temple of the Holy Ghost.

What is the length of this Temple?

From North to South.

What is the breadth of this Temple?

From East to West.

What is the height of this Temple?

From the Abyss to the Abyss.

There is, therefore, nothing movable or immovable under the whole firmament of heaven which is not included in this pantacle, though it be but " eight inches in diameter, and in thickness half an inch."

Fire is not matter at all; water is a combination of elements; air almost entirely a mixture of elements; earth contains all both in admixture and in combination.

So must it be with this Pantacle, the symbol of earth.

And as this Pantacle is made of pure wax, do not forget that "everything that lives is holy."

All phenomena are sacraments. Every fact, and even every falsehood, must enter into the Pantacle; it is the great storehouse from which the Magician draws.

" In the brown cakes of corn we shall taste the food of the world and be strong." [1]

---

[1] We have avoided dealing with the Pantacle as the Paten of the Sacrament, though special instructions about it are given in Liber Legis. It is composed of meal, honey, wine, holy oil, and blood.

When speaking of the Cup, it was shown how every fact must be made significant, how every stone must have its proper place in the mosaic. Woe were it were one stone misplaced! But that mosaic cannot be wrought at all, well or ill, unless every stone be there.

These stones are the simple impressions or experiences; not one may be foregone.

Do not refuse anything merely because you know that it is the cup of poison offered by your enemy; drink it with confidence; it is he that will fall dead!

How can I give Cambodian art its proper place in art, if I have never heard of Cambodia? How can the Geologist estimate the age of what lies beneath the chalk unless he have a piece of knowledge totally unconnected with geology, the life-history of the animals of whom that chalk is the remains?

This then is a very great difficulty for the Magician. He cannot possibly have all experience, and though he may console himself philosophically with the reflection that the Universe is conterminous with such experience as he has, he will find it grow at such a pace during the early years of his life that he may almost be tempted to believe in the possibility of experiences beyond his own, and from a practical standpoint he will seem to be confronted with so many avenues of knowledge that he will be bewildered which to choose.

The ass hesitated between two thistles; how much more that greater ass, that incomparably greater ass, between two thousand!

Fortunately it does not matter very much; but he should at least choose those branches of knowledge which abut directly upon universal problems.

He should choose not one but several, and these should be as diverse as possible in nature.

It is important that he should strive to excel in some sport, and that that sport should be the one best calculated to keep his body in health.

He should have a thorough grounding in classics, mathematics and science; also enough general knowledge of modern languages and of the shifts of life to enable him to travel in any part of the world with ease and security.

History and geography he can pick up as he wants them; and what should interest him most in any subject is its links with some other subject, so that his Pantacle may not lack what painters call "composition."

He will find that, however good his memory may be, ten thousand impressions enter his mind for every one that it is able to retain even for a day. And the excellence of a memory lies in the wisdom of its selection.

The best memories so select and judge that practically

nothing is retained which has not some coherence with the general plan of the mind.

All Pantacles will contain the ultimate conceptions of the circle and the cross, though some will prefer to replace the cross by a point, or by a Tau, or by a triangle. The Vesica Piscis is sometimes used instead of the circle, or the circle may be glyphed as a serpent. Time and space and the idea of causality are sometimes represented; so also are the three stages in the history of philosophy, in which the three objects of study were successively Nature, God, and Man.

The duality of consciousness is also sometimes represented; and the Tree of Life itself may be figured therein, or the categories. An emblem of the Great Work should be added. But the Pantacle will be imperfect unless each idea is contrasted in a balanced manner with its opposite, and unless there is a necessary connection between each pair of ideas and every other pair.

The Neophyte will perhaps do well to make the first sketches for his Pantacle very large and complex, subsequently simplifying, not so much by exclusion as by combination, just as a Zoologist, beginning with the four great Apes and Man, combines all in the single word "primate."

It is not wise to simplify too far, since the ultimate hieroglyphic must be an infinite. The ultimate resolution not having been performed, its symbol must not be portrayed.

If any person were to gain access to V.V.V.V.V.,[1] and ask Him to discourse upon any subject, there is little doubt that He could only comply by an unbroken silence, and even that might not be wholly satisfactory, since the Tao Teh King says that the Tao cannot be declared either by silence or by speech.

In this preliminary task of collecting materials, the idea of the Ego is not of such great moment; all impressions are phases of the non-ego, and the Ego serves merely as a receptacle. In fact, to the well regulated mind, there is no question but that the impressions are real, and that the mind, if not a *tabula rasa*, is only not so because of the "tendencies" or "innate ideas" which prevent some ideas from being received as readily as others.[2]

These "tendencies" must be combated: distasteful facts should be insisted upon until the Ego is perfectly indifferent to the nature of its food.

"Even as the diamond shall glow red for the rose, and green for the rose-leaf, so shalt thou abide apart from the Impressions."

This great task of separating the self from the impressions or "vrit-

---

[1] The Motto of the Chief of the A.·. A.·., "the Light of the World Himself."

[2] It does not occur to a newly-hatched chicken to behave in the same way as a new-born child.

tis" is one of the many meanings of the aphorism "solvé," corresponding to the "coagula" implied in Samadhi, and this **Pantacle** therefore
represents **all that we are**, the resultant of **all that we had
a tendency to be.**

In the Dhammapada we read:

All that we are from mind results; on mind is founded, built of mind;
Who acts or speaks with evil thought him doth pain follow sure and blind.
So the ox plants his foot, and so the car wheel follows hard behind.

All that we are from mind results; on mind is founded, built of mind;
Who acts or speaks with righteous thought him happiness doth surely find.
So failing not the shadow falls for ever in its place assigned.

The Pantacle is then in a sense identical with the Karma or Kamma
of the Magician.

The Karma of a man is his *ledger*. The balance has not been struck,
and he does not know what it is; he does not even fully know what
debts he may have to pay, or what is owed him; nor does he know on
what dates even those payments which he anticipates may fall due.

A business conducted on such lines would be in a terrible mess; and
we find in fact that man is in just such a mess. While he is working
day and night at some unimportant detail of his affairs, some giant
force may be advancing *pede claudo* to overtake him.

Many of the entries in this " ledger " are for the ordinary man necessarily illegible; the method of reading them is given in that important instruction of the A.·.A.·. called " Thisharb," Liber CMXIII.

Now consider that this Karma is all that a man has or is. His ultimate object is to get rid of it completely—when it comes to the point of surrendering[1] the Self to the Beloved; but in the beginning the Magician is not that Self, he is only the heap of refuse from which that Self is to be built up. The Magical instruments must be made before they are destroyed.

This idea of Karma has been confused by many who ought to have known better, including the Buddha, with the ideas of poetic justice and of retribution.

We have the story of one of the Buddha's Arahats, who being blind, in walking up and down unwittingly killed a number of insects. [The Buddhist regards the destruction of life as the most shocking crime.] His brother Arahats inquired as to how this was, and Buddha spun them a long yarn as to how, in a previous incarnation, he had maliciously deprived a woman of her sight. This is only a fairy tale, a bogey to frighten the children, and probably the worst way of influencing the young yet devised by human stupidity.

[1] To surrender all, one must give up not only the bad but the good; not only weakness but strength. How can the mystic surrender all, while he clings to his virtues?

Karma does not work in this way at all.

In any case moral fables have to be very carefully constructed, or they may prove dangerous to those who use them.

You will remember Bunyan's Passion and Patience: naughty Passion played with all his toys and broke them, good little Patience put them carefully aside. Bunyan forgets to mention that by the time Passion had broken all his toys, he had outgrown them.

Karma does not act in this tit-for-tat way. An eye for an eye is a sort of savage justice, and the idea of justice in our human sense is quite foreign to the constitution of the Universe.

Karma is the **Law of Cause and Effect.** There is no proportion in its operations. Once an accident occurs it is impossible to say what may happen; and the Universe is a stupendous accident.

We go out to tea a thousand times without mishap, and the thousand-and-first time we meet some one who changes radically the course of our lives for ever.

There is a sort of sense in which every impression that is made upon our minds is the resultant of all the forces of the past; no incident is so trifling that it has not in some way shaped one's disposition. But there is none of this crude retribution about it. One may kill a hundred thousand lice in one brief hour at the foot of the Baltoro Glacier, as Frater P. once did. It would be stupid to suppose, as the Theosophist inclines to suppose, that this action involves one in the doom of being killed by a louse a hundred thousand times.

This ledger of Karma is kept separate from the petty cash account; and in respect of bulk this petty cash account is very much bigger than the ledger.

If we eat too much salmon we get indigestion and perhaps nightmare. It is silly to suppose that a time will come when a salmon will eat us, and find us disagree.

On the other hand we are always being terribly punished for actions that are not faults at all. Even our virtues rouse insulted nature to revenge.

Karma only grows by what it feeds on: and if Karma is to be properly brought up, it requires a very careful diet.

With the majority of people their actions cancel each other out; no sooner is effort made than it is counterbalanced by idleness. Eros gives place to Anteros.

Not one man in a thousand makes even an apparent escape from the commonplace of animal life.

> Birth is sorrow;
> Life is sorrow;
> Sorrowful are old age, disease, and death;
> But resurrection is the greatest misery of all.

"Oh what misery! birth incessantly!" as Buddha said.

One goes on from day to day with a little of this and a little of that, a few kind thoughts and a few unkind thoughts; nothing really gets done. Body and mind are changed, changed beyond recall by nightfall. But what *meaning* has any of this change?

How few there are who can look back through the years and say that they have made advance in any definite direction? And in how few is that change, such as it is, a variable with intelligence and conscious volition! The dead weight of the original conditions under which we were born has counted for far more than all our striving. The unconscious forces are incomparably greater than those of which we have any knowledge. This is the *solidity* of our Pantacle, the Karma of our earth that whirls us will he nill he around her axis at the rate of a thousand miles an hour. And a thousand is Aleph, a capital Aleph, the microcosm of all-wandering air, the fool of the Taro, the aimlessness and fatality of things!

It is very difficult then in any way to *fashion* this heavy Pantacle.

We can engrave characters upon it with the dagger, but they will scarcely come to more than did the statue of Ozymandias, King of Kings, in the midst of the unending desert.

We cut a figure on the ice; it is effaced in a morning by the tracks of other skaters; nor did that figure do more than scratch the surface of the ice, and the ice itself must melt before the sun. Indeed the Magician may despair when he comes to make the Pantacle! Everyone has the material, one man's pretty well as good as his brothers; but for that Pantacle to be in any way fashioned to a willed end, or even to an intelligible end, or even to a known end: "Hoc opus, Hic labor est." It is indeed the toil of ascending from Avernus, and escaping to the upper air.

In order to do it, it is most necessary to understand our tendencies, and to will the development of one, the destruction of another. And though all elements in the Pantacle must ultimately be destroyed, yet some will help us directly to reach a position from which this task of destruction becomes possible; and there is no element therein which may not be occasionally helpful.

And so—beware! Select! Select! Select!

This Pantacle is an infinite storehouse; things will always be there when we want them. We may see to it occasionally that they are dusted and the moth kept out, but we shall usually be too busy to do much more. Remember that in travelling from the earth to the stars, one dare not be encumbered with too much heavy luggage. Nothing that is not a necessary part of the machine should enter into its composition.

Now though this Pantacle is composed only of shams, some shams somehow seem to be more false than others.

The whole Universe is an illusion, but it is an illusion difficult to get rid of. It is true compared with most things. But ninety-nine out of every hundred impressions are false even in relation to the things on their own plane.

Such distinctions must be graven deeply upon the surface of the Pantacle by the Holy Dagger.

There is only one other of the elemental Instruments to be considered, namely the Lamp.

THE LAMP

CHAPTER X

THE LAMP

IN Liber A. vel Armorum, the official instruction of the A. · A. for the preparation of the elemental weapons, it is said that each symbolic representation of the Universe is to be approved by the Superior of the Magician. To this rule the Lamp is an exception; it is said:

"A Magical Lamp that shall burn without wick or oil, being fed by the Aethyr. This shall he accomplish secretly and apart, without asking the advice or approval of his Adeptus Minor."

This **Lamp is the light of the pure soul**; it hath no need of fuel, it is the Burning Bush inconsumable that Moses saw, the image of the Most High.

This Lamp hangeth above the Altar, it hath no support from below; its light illumines the whole Temple, yet upon it are cast no shadows, no reflections. It cannot be touched, it cannot be extinguished, in no way can it change; for it is utterly apart from all those things which have complexity, which have dimension, which change and may be changed.

When the eyes of the Magus are fixed upon this Lamp naught else exists.

The Instruments lie idle on the Altar; that Light alone burns eternally.

The Divine Will that was the Wand is no more; for the path has become one with the Goal.

The Divine Understanding that was the Cup is no more; for the subject and Object of intelligence are one.

The Divine Reason that was the Sword is no more; for the complex has been resolved into the Simple.

And the Divine Substance that was the Pantacle is no more; for the many has become the One.

Eternal, unconfined, unextended, without cause and without effect, the Holy Lamp mysteriously burns. Without quantity or quality, un-conditioned and sempiternal, is this Light.

It is not possible for anyone to advise or approve; for this Lamp is not made with hands; it exists alone for ever; it has no parts, no person; it is before "I am." Few can behold it, yet it is always there. For it there is no *here* nor *there*, no *then* nor *now*; all parts of speech are abolished, save the noun; and this noun is not found either in human speech or in Divine. It is the Lost Word, the dying music of whose sevenfold echo is I A O and A U M. Without this Light the Magician could not work at all; yet few indeed are the Magicians that have known of it, and far fewer They that have beheld its brilliance!

The Temple and all that is in it must be destroyed again and again before it is worthy to receive that Light. Hence it so often seems that the only advice that any master can give to any pupil is to destroy the Temple.

Whatever you have and *whatever you are* are veils before that Light.

Yet in so great a matter all advice is vain. There is no master so great that he can see clearly the whole character of any pupil. What helped him in the past may hinder another in the future.

Yet since the Master is pledged to serve, he may take up that service on these simple lines. Since all thoughts are veils of this Light, he may advise the destruction of all thoughts, and to that end teach those practices which are clearly conducive to such destruction.

These practices have now fortunately been set down in clear language by order of the A∴ A∴

In these instructions the relativity and limitation of each practice is clearly taught, and all dogmatic interpretations are carefully avoided.

Each practice is in itself a demon which must be destroyed; but to be destroyed it must first be evoked.

Shame upon that Master who shirks any one of these practices, however distasteful or useless it may be to him! For in the detailed knowledge of it, which experience alone can give him, may lie his opportunity for crucial assistance to a pupil. However dull the drudgery, it should be undergone. If it were possible to regret anything in life, which is fortunately not the case, it would be the hours wasted in fruitful practices which might have been more profitably employed on sterile ones: for NEMO [1] in tending his garden seeketh not to single out the flower that shall be NEMO after him. And we are not told that NEMO might have used other things than those which he actually does use; it seems possible that if he had not the acid or the knife, or the fire, or the oil, he might miss tending just that one flower which was to be NEMO after him!

[1] NEMO is the Master of the Temple, whose task it is to develop the beginner. See Liber CDXVIII, Aethyr XIII.

THE CROWN

CHAPTER XI

THE Crown of the Magician represents the Attainment of his Work. It is a band of pure gold, on the front of which stand three pentagrams, and on the back a hexagram. The central pentagram contains a diamond or a great opal; the other three symbols contain the Tau. Around this Crown is twined the golden Uraeus serpent, with erect head and expanded hood. Under the Crown is a crimson cap of maintenance, which falls to the shoulders.

Instead of this, the Ateph Crown of Thoth is sometimes worn; for Thoth is the God of Truth, of Wisdom, and the Teacher of Magick. The Ateph Crown has two ram's horns, showing energy, dominion, the force that breaks down obstacles, the sign of the spring. Between these horns is the disk of the sun; from this springs a Lotus upheld by the twin plumes of truth, and three other sun-disks are upheld, one by the cup of the lotus, the others beneath the curving feathers.

There is still another Crown, the Crown of Amoun, the concealed one, from whom the Hebrews borrowed their holy word "Amen." This Crown consists simply of the plumes of truth. But into the symbolism of these it is not necessary to go, for all this and more is in the Crown first described.

The crimson cap implies concealment, and is also symbolical of the flood of glory that pours upon the Magician from above. It is of velvet for the softness of that divine kiss, and crimson for that it is the very blood of God which is its life. The band of gold is the eternal circle of perfection. The three pentagrams symbolize the Father, the Son, and the Holy Spirit, while the hexagram represents the Magician himself. Ordinarily, pentagrams represent the microcosm, hexagrams the macrocosm; but here the reverse is the case, because in this Crown of Perfection, that which is below has become that which is above, and that which is above has become that which is below. If a diamond be worn, it is for the Light which is before all manifestations in form; if an opal, it is to commemorate that sublime plan of the All, to fold and unfold in eternal rapture, to manifest as the Many that the Many may become the One Unmanifest. But this matter is too great for an elementary treatise on Magick.

The Serpent which is coiled about the Crown means many things, or, rather, one thing in many ways. It is the symbol of royalty and of initiation, for the Magician is anointed King and Priest.

It also represents Hadit, of which one can here only quote these words: " I am the secret serpent coiled about to spring; in my coiling there is joy. If I lift up my head, I and my Nuit are one; if I droop down mine head and shoot forth venom, there is rapture of the earth, and I and the earth are one."

The serpent is also the Kundalini serpent, the Magical force itself, the manifesting side of the Godhead of the Magician, whose unmanifested side is peace and silence, of which there is no symbol.

In the Hindu system the Great Work is represented by saying that this serpent, which is normally coiled at the base of the spine, rises with her hood over the head of the Yogi, there to unite with the Lord of all.

The serpent is also he who poisons. It is that force which destroys the manifested Universe. This is also the emerald snake which encircles the Universe. This matter must be studied in Liber LXV, where this is discussed incomparably. In the hood of this serpent are the six jewels, three on each side, Ruby, Emerald, and Sapphire, the three holy elements made perfect, on both sides in equilibrium.

THE ROBE

CHAPTER XII

THE Robe of the Magician may be varied according to his grade and the nature of his working.

There are two principal Robes, the white and the black; of these the black is more important than the white, for the white has no hood. These Robes may be varied by the addition of various symbols, but in any case the shape of the Robe is a Tau.

The general symbolism which we have adopted leads us, however, to prefer the description of a Robe which few dare wear. This Robe is of a rich silk of deep pure blue, the blue of the night sky: it is embroidered with golden stars, and with roses and lilies. Around the hem, its tail in its mouth, is the great serpent, while upon the front from neck to hem falls the Arrow described in the Vision of the Fifth Aethyr. This Robe is lined with purple silk on which is embroidered a green serpent coiled from neck to hem. The symbolism of this Robe treats of high mysteries

which must be studied in Liber CCXX and Liber CDXVIII; but
having thus dealt with special Robes, let us consider the use of the
Robe in general.

**The Robe is that which conceals, and which protects the
Magician from the elements; it is the silence and secrecy
with which he works, the hiding of himself in the occult
life of Magick and Meditation.** This is the "going away into the
wilderness" which we find in the lives of all men of the highest types
of greatness. And it is also the withdrawing of one's self from life as
such.

In another sense it is the "Aura" of the Magician, that invisible egg
or sheath which surrounds him. This "Aura" must be shining, elastic,
impenetrable, even by the light, that is, by any partial light that comes
from one side.

The only light of the Magician is from the Lamp which hangs above
his head, as he stands in the centre of the Circle, and the Robe, being
open at the neck, opposes no obstacles to the passage of this light.
And being open, and very wide open, at the bottom, it permits that
light to pass and illumine them that sit in darkness and in the shadow
of death.

THE BOOK

CHAPTER XIII

THE BOOK

THE Book of Spells or of Conjurations is the Record of every thought, word, and deed of the Magician; for everything that he has willed is willed to a purpose. It is the same as if he had taken an oath to perform some achievement.

Now this Book must be a holy Book, not a scribbling-book in which you jot down every piece of rubbish that comes into your head. It is written, Liber VII, v, 23: " Every breath, every word, every thought, every deed is an act of love with Thee. Be this devotion a potent spell to exorcise the demons of the Five."

This Book must then be thus written. In the first place the Magician must perform the practice laid down in Liber CMXIII so that he understands perfectly who he is, and to what his development must necessarily tend. So much for the first page of the Book.

Let him then be careful to write nothing therein that is

inharmonious or untrue. Nor can he avoid this writing, for this is a Magick Book. If you abandon even for an hour the one purpose of your life, you will find a number of meaningless scratches and scrawls on the white vellum; and these cannot be erased. In such a case, when you come to conjure a demon by the power of the Book, he will mock you; he will point to all this foolish writing, more like his own than yours. In vain will you continue with the subsequent spells; you have broken by your own foolishness the chain which would have bound him.

Even the calligraphy of the Book must be firm, clear, and beautiful; in the cloud of incense it is hard to read the conjurations. While you peer dimly through the smoke, the demon will vanish, and you will have to write the terrible word " failure."

And yet there is no page of this Book on which this word is not written; but so long as it is immediately followed by a new affirmation, all is not lost; and as in this Book the word " failure " is thus made of little account, so also must the word "success" never be employed, for it is the last word that may be written therein, and it is followed by a full stop.

This full stop may never be written anywhere else; for the writing of the Book goes on eternally; there is no way of closing the record until the goal of all has been attained. Let every page of this Book be filled with song—for it is a Book of incantation!

The pages of this Book are of virgin vellum, made from the calf which was borne by Isis-Hathor the Great Mother, to Osiris-Apis the Redeemer. It is bound in blue leather on which the word *Thelema* is written in gold. Let the pen with which the writing is done be the feather of a young male swan—that swan whose name is Aum. And let the ink be made of the gall of a fish, the fish Oannes.

Thus far concerning the Book.

THE BELL

CHAPTER XIV

THE BELL

THE Magical Bell is best attached to the chain. In some systems of Magick a number of bells have been worn, sewn upon the hem of the robe with the idea of symbolizing that every movement of the Magician should make music. But the Bell of which we shall speak is a more important implement. This Bell summons and alarms; and it is also the Bell which sounds at the elevation of the Host.

It is thus also the " Astral Bell " of the Magician.[1]

The Bell of which we speak is a disk of some two inches in diameter, very slightly bent into a shape not unlike that of a cymbal. A hole in the centre permits the passage of a short leather thong, by which it may

[1] During certain meditation-practices the Student hears a bell resound in the depths of his being. It is not subjective, for it is scmetimes heard by other people. Some Magicians are able to call the attention of those with whom they wish to communicate at a distance by its means, or, so it is said.

be attached to the chain. At the other end of the chain is the striker; which, in Tibet, is usually made of human bone.

The Bell itself is made of electrum magicum, an alloy of the "seven metals" blended together in a special manner. First the gold is melted up with the silver during a favourable aspect of the sun and moon; these are then fused with tin when Jupiter is well dignified. Lead is added under an auspicious Saturn; and so for the quicksilver, copper, and iron, when Mercury, Venus, and Mars are of good augury.

The sound of this Bell is indescribably commanding, solemn, and majestic. Without even the minutest jar, its single notes tinkle fainter and fainter into silence. **At the sound of this Bell the Universe ceases for an indivisible moment of time, and attends to the Will of the Magician.** Let him not interrupt the sound of this Bell. Let this be that which is written, Liber VII, v, 31: "There is a solemnity of the silence. There is no more voice at all."

As the Magical Book was the record of the past, so is the Magick Bell the prophecy of the future. The manifested shall repeat itself again and again, always a clear thin note, always a simplicity of music, yet ever less and less disturbing the infinite silence until the end.

THE LAMEN

EXAMPLE OF DESIGN FOR A LAMEN

CHAPTER XV

THE LAMEN

THE breastplate or Lamen of the Magician is a very elaborate and important symbol. In the Jewish system we read that the High Priest was to wear a plate with twelve stones, for the twelve tribes of Israel (with all their correspondences), and in this plate were kept the Urim and Thummim.[1]

The modern Lamen is, however, a simple plate which (being worn over the heart) symbolizes Tiphereth, and it should therefore be a harmony of all the other symbols in one. It connects naturally by its shape with the Circle and the Pentacle; but it is not sufficient to repeat the design of either.

The Lamen of the spirit whom one wishes to evoke is both placed in the triangle and worn on the breast; but in this case, since that

---

[1] Scholars are uncertain as to what these really were, though apparently they were methods of divination.

which we wish to evoke is nothing partial, but whole, we shall have but a single symbol to combine the two. **The Great Work will then form the subject of the design.**[1]

In this Lamen the Magician must place the secret keys of his power.

The Pentacle is merely the material to be worked upon, gathered together and harmonized but not yet in operation, the parts of the engine arranged for use, or even put together, but not yet set in motion. In the Lamen these forces are already at work; even accomplishment is prefigured.

In the system of Abramelin the Lamen is a plate of silver upon which the Holy Guardian Angel writes in dew. This is another way of expressing the same thing, for it is He who confers the secrets of that power which should be herein expressed. St. Paul expresses the same thing when he says that the breastplate is faith, and can withstand the fiery darts of the wicked. This "faith" is not blind self-confidence

[1] Some writers have actually confused the Lamen with the Pantacle, usually through a misunderstanding of the nature of the latter. Dr. Dee's "Sigillum Dei Amath" makes a fine pantacle, but it would be useless as a lamen. Eliphas Levi made several attempts to draw one or the other, he never seemed sure which. Fortunately he knows better now. The lamens given in the Lesser and Greater Keys of "Solomon" are rather better, but we know of no perfect example. The design on the cover of "The Star in the West" represents an early effort of Fra. P.

and credulity; it is that self-confidence which only comes when self is forgotten.

It is the " Knowledge and Conversation of the Holy Guardian Angel" which confers this faith. The task of attaining to this Knowledge and Conversation is the sole task of him who would be called Adept. An absolute method for achieving this is given in the Eighth Aethyr (Liber CDXVIII, Equinox V).

THE MAGICK FIRE

THE CENSER (CROWLEY'S PATENT PATTERN).

CHAPTER XVI

THE MAGICK FIRE; WITH CONSIDERATIONS OF THE THURIBLE, THE CHARCOAL, AND THE INCENSE

INTO the Magick Fire all things are cast. It symbolizes the final burning up of all things in Shivadarshana. It is the absolute destruction alike of the Magician and the Universe.

The Thurible stands upon a small altar. "My altar is of open brass-work; burn thereon in silver or gold." This altar stands in the East, as if to symbolize the identity of Hope and Annihilation. This brass contains the metals of Jupiter and Venus fused in a homogeneous alloy. This is then symbolical of divine love, and it is "open brass work" because this love is not limited in direction or extent; it is not particularized, it is universal.

Upon this altar stands the Censer proper; it has three legs symbolical of fire.[1] Its cup is a hemisphere, and supported from its edge

[1] Because Shin, the Hebrew letter of Fire, has three tongues of flame, and its value is 300.

is a plate pierced with holes. This Censer is of silver or gold, because these were called the perfect metals; it is upon perfection that the imperfect is burned. Upon this plate burns a great fire of charcoal, impregnated with nitre. This charcoal is (as chemists now begin to surmise) the ultimate protean element: absolutely black, because it absorbs all light; infusible by the application of any known heat; the lightest of those elements which occur in the solid state in nature; the essential constituent of all known forms of life.

It has been treated with nitre, whose potassium has the violet flame of Jupiter, the father of all, whose nitrogen is that inert element which by proper combination becomes a constituent of all the most explosive bodies known; and oxygen, the food of fire. This fire is blown upon by the Magician; this blaze of destruction has been kindled by his word and by his will.

Into this Fire he casts the Incense, symbolical of prayer, the gross vehicle or image of his aspiration. Owing to the imperfection of this image, we obtain mere smoke instead of perfect combustion. But we cannot use explosives instead of incense, because it would not be true. **Our prayer is the expression of the lower aspiring to the higher**; it is without the clear vision of the higher, it does not under stand what the higher wants. And, however sweet may be its smell, it is always cloudy.

In this smoke illusions arise. We sought the light, and behold the Temple is darkened! In the darkness this smoke seems to take strange shapes, and we may hear the crying of beasts. The thicker the smoke, the darker grows the Universe. We gasp and tremble, beholding what foul and unsubstantial things we have evoked!

Yet we cannot do without the Incense! Unless our aspiration took form it could not influence form. This also is the mystery of incarnation.

This Incense is based upon Gum Olibanum, the sacrifice of the human will of the heart. This olibanum has been mixed with half its weight of storax, the earthly desires, dark, sweet, and clinging; and this again with half its weight of lignum aloes, which symbolizes Sagittarius, the arrow,[1] and so represents the aspiration itself; it is the arrow that cleaves the rainbow. This arrow is " Temperance " in the Taro; it is a life equally balanced and direct which makes our work possible; yet this life itself must be sacrificed!

In the burning up of these things arise in our imagination those terrifying or alluring phantasms which throng the " Astral Plane." This smoke represents the " Astral Plane," which lies between the

---

[1] Note that there are two arrows: the Divine shot downward, the human upward. The former is the Oil, the latter the Incense, or rather the finest part of it. See Liber CDXVIII, Fifth Aethyr.

material and the spiritual. One may now devote a little attention to the consideration of this "plane," about which a great deal of nonsense has been written.

When a man shuts his eyes and begins to look about him, at first there is nothing but darkness. If he continues trying to penetrate the gloom, a new pair of eyes gradually opens.

Some people think that these are the "eyes of imagination." Those with more experience understand that this truly represents things seen, although those things are themselves totally false.

At first the seer will perceive gray gloom; in subsequent experiments perhaps figures may appear with whom the seer may converse, and under whose guidance he may travel about. This "plane" being quite as large and varied as the material Universe, one cannot describe it effectively; we must refer the reader to Liber O and to Equinox II, pages 295 to 334.

This "Astral Plane" has been described by Homer in the Odyssey. Here are Polyphemus and the Laestrygons, here Calypso and the Sirens. Here, too, are those things which many have imagined to be the "spirits" of the dead. If the student once take any of these things for truth, he must worship it, since all truth is worshipful. In such a case he is lost; the phantom will have power over him; it will obsess him.

As long as an idea is being examined you are free from

it. There is no harm in a man's experimenting with opium-smoking or feeding on nuts; but the moment he ceases to examine, to act from habit and without reflection, he is in trouble. We all of us eat too much, because people, liveried and obsequious, have always bustled up five times daily with six months' provisions, and it was less trouble to feed and be done with it, than to examine the question whether we were hungry. If you cook your own food, you soon find that you don't cook more or less than you want; and health returns. If, however, you go to the other extreme and think of nothing but diet, you are almost sure to acquire that typical form of melancholia, in which the patient is convinced that all the world is in league to poison him. Professor Schweinhund has shown that beef causes gout; Professor Naschtikoff proves that milk causes consumption. Sir Ruffon Wratts tells us that old age is brought on by eating cabbage. By and by you reach the state of which Mr. Hereward Carrington makes his proud boast: your sole food is chocolate, which you chew unceasingly, even in your dreams. Yet no sooner have you taken it into you than you awake to the terrible truth demonstrated by Guterbock Q. Hosenscheisser, Fourth Avenue, Grand Rapids, that chocolate is the cause of constipation, and constipation of cancer, and proceed to get it out of you by means of an enema which would frighten a camel into convulsions.

A similar madness attacks even real men of science. Metchnikoff studied the diseases of the colon until he could see nothing else, and then calmly proposed to cut out every one's colon, pointing out that a vulture (who has no colon) is a very long-lived bird. As a matter of fact the longevity of the vulture is due to its twisted neck, and many thoughtful persons propose to experiment on Professor Metchnikoff.

But **the worst of all phantasms are the moral ideas and the religious ideas.** Sanity consists in the faculty of adjusting ideas in proper proportion. Any one who accepts a moral or religious truth without understanding it is only kept out of the asylum because he does not follow it out logically. If one really believed in Christianity,[1] if one really thought that the majority of mankind was doomed to eternal punishment, one would go raving about the world trying to "save" people. Sleep would not be possible until the horror of the mind left the body exhausted. Otherwise, one must be morally insane. Which of us can sleep if one we love is in danger of mere death? We cannot even see a dog drown without at least interrupting all our business to look on. Who then can live in London and reflect upon the fact that of its seven million souls, all but about a thousand Plymouth Brethren will be damned? Yet the thousand Plymouth Brethren (who are the loudest in proclaiming that they will be the only ones saved) seem to

---

[1] " One would go mad if one took the Bible seriously; but to take it seriously one must be already mad."—*Crowley.*

get on very well, thank you. Whether they are hypocrites or morally insane is a matter which we can leave to their own consideration.

All these phantoms, of whatever nature, must be evoked, examined, and mastered; otherwise we may find that just when we want it there is some idea with which we have never dealt; and perhaps that idea, springing on us by surprise, and as it were from behind, may strangle us. This is the legend of the sorcerer strangled by the Devil!

GLOSSARY

GLOSSARY

ONLY words nowhere explained in the preceding pages are given in this list. Several others, mentioned in passing in the early part of the book, are sufficiently dealt with later on. In these cases the references in the Index should be turned up.

A ∴ A ∴. The Great White Brotherhood which is giving this Method of Attainment to the world. *See* Equinox I.

Adeptus Minor. A grade of adeptship. *See* Equinox III.

Aethyrs. See Equinox V and VII.

Aima. The Great Fertile Mother Nature.

Ama. The Great Mother not yet fertile.

Amoun. The God Amen = Zeus = Jupiter, etc., etc.

Ankh. The Symbol of "Life." A form of the Rosy Cross. *See* Equinox III.

Apophis. The Serpent-God who slew Osiris. *See* Equinox III.

Babalon, Our Lady. See Equinox V, The Vision and the Voice, 14th Aethyr.

Babe of the Abyss. See Equinox VIII, Temple of Solomon.

Bhagavadgita. Sacred Hymn of India, translated by Sir Edwin Arnold in the "Song Celestial."

Binah. Understanding, the 3rd "emanation" of the Absolute.

Caduceus. The Wand of Mercury. *See* Equinox II and III.

175

Chela. Pupil.

Chesed. Mercy, the 4th "emanation" of the Absolute.

Chokmah. Wisdom, the 2nd "emanation" of the Absolute.

Choronzon. *See* Equinox V, The Vision and the Voice, 10th Aethyr.

City of the Pyramids. *See* Equinox V, The Vision and the Voice, 14th Aethyr.

Crux Ansata. Same as Ankh, *q.v.*

Daäth. Knowledge, child of Chokmah and Binah in one sense; in another, the home of Choronzon.

Dhammapada. A sacred Buddhist book.

Elemental Kings. *See* 777.

Geburah. Strength, the 5th "emanation" of the Absolute.

Gunas. Three principles. *See* Bhagadvadgita, 777, etc.

Guru. Teacher.

Hadit. *See* "Liber Legis," Equinox VII. Also "Liber 555."

Hathayoga Pradipika. A book on physical training for spiritual purposes.

Hod. Splendour, the 8th "emanation" of the Absolute.

Kamma. Pali dialect of Karma, *q.v.*

Karma. "That which is made," "The law of cause and effect." *See* "Science and Buddhism," Crowley, Coll. Works, Vol. II.

Kether. The Crown, 1st "emanation" of the Absolute.

Lao Tze. Great Chinese teacher, founder of Taoists. *See* Tao Teh King.

Liber Legis. *See* Equinox VII for facsimile reproduction of MS.

Lingam. The Unity or Male Principle. But these have many symbols, *e.g.*, sometimes Yoni is o or 3 and Lingam 2.

Lingam-Yoni. A form of the Rosy Cross.

Macrocosm. The great Universe, of which man is an exact image.

Magus. A magician. Technically, also, a Master of grade $9^{\circ}=2^{\circ}$. *See* Equinox VII, " Liber I," and elsewhere.

Mahalingam. See Lingam. Maha means great.

Maha Sattipatthana. A mode of meditation. *See* " Science and Buddhism," Crowley, Coll. Works, Vol. II, for a full account.

Malkah. A young girl. The " bride." The unredeemed soul.

Malkuth. " The kingdom," 10th " emanation " of the Absolute.

Mantrayoga. A practice to attain union with God by repetition of a sacred sentence.

Master of the Temple. One of grade $8^{\circ}=3^{\circ}$. Fully discussed in Equinox.

Microcosm. Man, considered as an exact image of the Universe.

Nephesch. The " animal soul " of man.

Netzach. Victory, the 7th " emanation " of the Absolute.

Nibbana. The state called, for want of a better name, annihilation. The final goal.

Nirvana. See Nibbana.

Nuit. See " Liber Legis."

Paths. See 777, and Equinox II and elsewhere.

Perdurabo, Frater. See Equinox I-X, " The Temple of Solomon the King."

Prana. See " Raja Yoga."

Qabalah. See "The tradition of secret wisdom of the Hebrews," Equinox V
Qliphoth. "Shells" or demons. The excrement of ideas.

Ra-Hoor-Khuit. See "Liber Legis."
Ruach. The intellect and other mental qualities. *See* 777, etc.

Sahasrara Cakkra. "The Temple of Solomon the King." *See* Equinox IV.
Sammasati. See "The Training of the Mind," Equinox V, and "The Temple
of Solomon," Equinox VIII. *Also* "Science and Buddhism," Crowley,
Coll. Works, Vol. II.
Sankhara. See "Science and Buddhism."
Sanna. See "Science and Buddhism."
Sephiroth. See "Temple of Solomon," Equinox V.
Shin. "A tooth." Hebrew letter = Sh, corresponds to Fire and Spirit.
Shiva Sanhita. A Hindu treatise on physical training for spiritual ends.
Skandhas. See "Science and Buddhism."

Tao. See Konx Om Pax, "Thien Tao," 777, etc.
Tao Teh King. Chinese Classic on the Tao.
Taro. See 777, Equinox III and VIII, etc., etc.
Tau. A "cross," Hebrew letter = Th corresponds to "Earth." *See* 777.
Thaumiel. The demons corresponding to Kether. Two contending forces.
Theosophist. A person who talks about Yoga, and does no work.
Thoth. The Egyptian god of Speech, Magick, Wisdom.
Tiphereth. "Beauty" or "Harmony," the 6th "emanation" of the Absolute.
Typhon. The destroyer of Osiris.

Udana. One of the imaginary "nerves" of Hindu pseudo-physiology.

Vedana. *See* " Science and Buddhism," Crowley, Coll. Works, Vol. II.

Vesica, Vesica Piscis. *See* Yoni. The oval formed by the intersection of the circles in Euclid 1, 1.

Virakam, Soror. A chela of Frater Perdurabo.

Vrittis. " Impressions."

Yesod. " Foundation," the ninth " emanation " of the Absolute.

Yogi. One who seeks to attain " Union " (with God). A Hindu word corresponding to the Mohammedan word Fakir.

Yoni. The Dyad, or Female Principle. *See* Lingam.

Zohar. Splendour, a collection of books on the Qabalah. *See* " The Temple of Solomon the King," Equinox V.

NOTICE

The A∴ A∴ is an organization whose heads have obtained by personal experience to the summit of this science. They have founded a system by which every one can equally attain, and that with an ease and speed which was previously impossible.

The first grade in Their system is that of

STUDENT.

A Student must possess the following books:

1. The Equinox, No. I to the current number.
2. 777. 10s.
3. Konx Om Pax. 10s.
4. Collected Works of A. Crowley; Tannhäuser, The Sword of Song, Time, Eleusis. 3 vols, £2 2s.
5. Raja Yoga, by Swami Vivekananda. 3s. 6d.
6. The Shiva Sanhita, or the Hathayoga Pradipika. 5s.
7. The Tao Teh King and the writings of Kwang Tze: S.B.E. xxxix, xl. 15s.

8. The Spiritual Guide, by Miguel de Molinos. 1*s.*

9. Rituel et Dogme de la Haute Magie, by Eliphas Lévi, or its translation by A. E. Waite. 7*s.* 6*d.*

10. The Goetia of the Lemegeton of Solomon the King. £1 1*s.*

Study of these books will give a thorough grounding in the intellectual side of Their system.

After three months the Student is examined in these books, and if his knowledge of them is found satisfactory, he may become a Probationer, receiving Liber LXI and the secret holy book, Liber LXV. The principal point of this grade is that the Probationer has a master appointed, whose experience can guide him in his work.

He may select any practices that he prefers, but in any case must keep an exact record, so that he may discover the relation of cause and effect in his working, and so that the A∴ A∴ may judge of his progress, and direct his further studies.

After a year of probation he may be admitted a Neophyte of the A∴ A∴, and receive the secret holy book Liber VII.

These are the principal instructions for practice which every probationer should follow out:

Libri E, A, O, III, XXX, CLXXV, CC, CCVI, CMXIII, while the Key to Magick Power is given in Liber CCCLXX.

Through the generosity of a colleague a sum of money has been provided to enable Messrs. Wieland to sell some of the books appointed for the Student at two-thirds of the published price to anyone who fills up and encloses the following form.

To WIELAND AND CO.,

33, AVENUE STUDIOS
(76, FULHAM ROAD),
SOUTH KENSINGTON,
LONDON, S.W.

I wish to enter my name as a Student of the Mysteries of A∴ A∴ Please forward me Items 1, 2, 3, 4, *and* 10, *in payment for which I enclose   for Six Guineas,* $31, *or* 156 *francs.*

Name ....

Address ....

....

Date ....

[This order can only be filled about fifty times more.]

ORDER FORM

Part III of this BOOK FOUR ["RITUAL"] *is in the Press, and will be published as early as possible. Three shillings net.*

Orders should be sent in at once to WIELAND AND CO., 33, AVENUE STUDIOS (76, FULHAM ROAD), SOUTH KENSINGTON, LONDON, S.W

Tel: 2632 KEN.

M∴ M∴ M∴

A Society to illustrate the principles of this book in practice has been formed. The method chosen is that of a series of Initiations.

Further practical instruction is given to Initiates according to their grade.

This School is in alliance with all the principal Bodies of High Grade Freemasonry.

Besides the Ceremonies of Initiation, there are a number of other Ceremonies to develop further instruction.

Fuller information may be obtained at a personal interview with the Grand Secretary General, to whom application should be made for an appointment. Such letters should be registered and addressed:

THE GRAND SECRETARY GENERAL, M.· M.∴ M.
33, AVENUE STUDIOS
(76, FULHAM ROAD),
SOUTH KENSINGTON, S.W.

Names of Degrees.				Fee for Initiation.		
Minerval	.	.	.	. £1	1	0
I° .	.	.	.	. 1		0
II°	.	.	.	.		0
III°	.	.	.	.		0
L. of P.	.	.	.	. 1	1	0
IV°	.	.	.	. 2	2	0
C. P. I. .	.	.	.	. 1	1	0
L. K. E. W. .	.	.	.	. _	_	0
V°	.	.	.	. 3	3	0

Details of Higher Grades communicated on further inquiry.

Printed in Great Britain
by Amazon